D1436088

DEER

DEER

•NORMA CHAPMAN•

with illustrations by
DIANA E. BROWN

Whittet Books

(End paper) *Alarmed young muntjac buck, bounding roe buck and pronking fallow buck.*

(Title page) *Fallow deer in a park in October, a rutting buck groans as he advances towards a rival.*

First published 1991
Text © 1991 by Norma Chapman
Illustrations © 1991 by Diana E. Brown
Whittet Books Ltd, 18 Anley Road, London W14 0BY

Design by Richard Kelly

The author and publishers are grateful for permission to reproduce the map on p.105 from Leonard Cantor's *Medieval Parks of England*.

British Library Cataloguing in Publication Data

Chapman, Norma
   Deer.
   1. Deer
   I. Title   II. Series
   599.7357

   ISBN 0–905483–88–X

Typeset by Litho Link Ltd, Welshpool, Powys, Wales
Printed in Great Britain by Biddles of Guildford

Contents

Preface

Deer have given me a great deal of satisfaction and I hope that this book will introduce this fascinating family of animals to many more observers. Once you know an area in which they are living, watching deer can be more predictable than observing many of our other wild mammals. Watching them in parks offers plenty of scope for seeing and recording their behaviour and the activities that make up a deer's year.

Members of the deer family have a very long history of association with and in the service of man. They deserve adequate protection and humane treatment. The more knowledge, understanding and appreciation of their needs people have, the more likely these are to be achieved.

Acknowledgments
The information in this book draws extensively on the published work of many people. To cite the references would make the text cumbersome and a list of all the publications would fill many pages. I can express only a blanket acknowledgment to them all. This is an opportunity to thank all who have worked with me over the years, in Essex, in Richmond Park and in the King's Forest, to the landowners and authorities responsible for those places, to all the stalkers who have allowed me access to carcases or preserved 'bits and pieces' for me and others who have salvaged carcases from roadsides. Over the years many co-researchers and others have given encouragement and advice. Friends in various countries have provided generous hospitality and enabled me to see different habitats and species of deer. Special thanks go to Stephen Harris, Kathie and Mick Claydon and Diane Blakeley who resolved that the field work on muntjac, then in its early phase, would continue after Donald's fatal accident. Their enthusiasm for deer, like mine, had been fostered by him. All of us in this team are very aware of the wonderful support given by so many for so long and without which the project could not have succeeded. My 'deer friends' span the alphabet, from artists and archaeologists to zoologists. It has been a great pleasure to work with Diana, who knows deer so well and has the rare talent to convey her observations so accurately. I shall miss her constant stream of illustrated letters and envelopes. I am grateful to Adrian Lister for consultation about fossil deer and to Kathie Claydon for commenting on the draft of the text.

Introduction

The opportunities for seeing deer in Britain are greater now than ever. Distribution of our native and introduced species continues to increase. Numerous parks are stocked with fallow and red deer, while some have sika; most wildlife parks and zoos have several species. The mushrooming of deer farms has brought red and fallow within the view, as well as the diet, of many more people.

In decreasing order of size, the deer established in the wild in Britain are the red, fallow, sika, roe, Chinese water deer and muntjac. Except for the water deer they are widely distributed. Visitors to the Cairngorms have the possibility of seeing reindeer roaming over the mountains. These seven species are but a few representatives of a large family, the Cervidae. Over forty species, and several times that number of sub-species, of the family are living today throughout the world. Some are threatened with extinction, the fate that befell Schomburgk's deer which lived in Thailand until about sixty years ago.

Deer of one sort or another occur in most of the major habitats from the bleak Arctic tundra to the lush tropical forests of Asia and South America, although as a family the deer are predominantly from the northern hemisphere. Not content with this distribution, man, for various reasons, has transported deer across the globe. No less then ten species were

'So you are a deer too!'

introduced to Australia and New Zealand which under nature's plan were deerless.

This book is not the place to compile a cervine *Who's Who* to show their diversity of form, adaptations and sizes which range from the diminutive pudu to the mighty moose. Nevertheless, the following maps and comments on some endangered species should give some insight into the variety of forms and life styles within the family. Other sections will refer briefly to species outside Britain where this is considered appropriate.

Why use Latin?

The deer with the scientific name of Alces alces *is known as the 'moose' in North America but is called the 'elk' in Scandinavia and Russia. The name 'elk' is used in North America, but for the deer which in Europe and Asia is called 'wapiti'. The 'reindeer' of northern Europe is the same species as the 'caribou' of North America, namely* Rangifer tarandus. *In Japan any reference to the 'spotted deer' means the 'sika',*

Cervus nippon, *but in India 'spotted deer' is another name for the 'axis deer', also called 'chital',* Axis axis. *The swamp deer of India,* Cervus duvauceli, *is often called by its native name of 'barasingha' (which means 12 points), but that name has been used for the Kashmir red deer, which has another name — 'hangul'.*

There are plenty more examples of deer having two or more English

"NO! I'M an ELK! You're a Moose."

"NO! I'M an ELK! You're a Wapiti."

AMERICA

SCOTLAND

SCANDINAVIA

"No! I'm a moose!!"

names. The only sure way for biologists worldwide to know which animal is being written about is to use its Latin name.

Within one family of animals, all the members have some features in common, such as, in the Cervidae, the possession of antlers (and/or tusks, which distinguish males from females) and the lack of a gall bladder. Not all members of a family are equally closely related, but when the relationship is very close this shows in the names they have been given. The first part of the name is the animal's genus (or generic name), and the second is its species (or specific name). Sometimes the same word is used for both of these names, as in the roe deer, Capreolus capreolus, whose larger cousin, the Siberian roe, is Capreolus pygargus. The fact that these two have the same first name shows that they are closely related; they are of the same genus but are different species.

In the case of deer very often there are several forms of a species, not sufficiently different to be split into separate species but distinct enough to be called sub-species. The European fallow deer is Dama dama dama: it just happens that in this example the same word is used for the generic, specific and sub-specific names. The Mesopotamian (or Persian) fallow is Dama dama mesopotamica. Just by looking at these names we can see that these

two are closely related, being two sub-species of fallow deer.

Chaos would reign among zoologists, botanists and gardeners without the universally adopted system of names which was introduced in the eighteenth century by the great Swedish naturalist, Carl Linnaeus. When a name and a date are written after a scientific name they indicate when and by whom the animal (or plant) was named. Those having L. or Linn. were described and named by Linnaeus himself.

Taxonomists, who study classification, sometimes decide that an animal is more, or less, closely related to another than previously thought. Thus, until recently, wapiti were named Cervus canadensis. Now all seven types of wapiti are regarded as large versions of red deer, Cervus elaphus, so bear these two names plus their own sub-species names.

Deer under threat

The decline in populations, even leading to extinction, is all too familiar a story for animals worldwide. Fortunately in Britain our deer species are thriving and are probably more numerous now than at any other time in history. Indeed, in Scotland the main problem of the red deer is overpopulation. However, on a global scale, over fifty species and sub-species of deer are regarded as endangered, vulnerable or rare (the three terms used to describe the status of threatened animals, the most threatened being 'endangered'). Restrictions on the killing of a species alone can achieve little success, partly because laws are so often difficult to enforce, but also because the habitat may no longer provide all the animals' requirements, in which case their long-term survival is doomed.

The International Union for the Conservation of Nature has a Deer Specialist Group which collates and disseminates information, advises and, when funds can be mustered, encourages projects directed towards conservation of the threatened species. Often very little is known of the basic natural history and requirements of these rare deer. The main problems are, as usual, associated with destruction or alteration of habitats and over-exploitation. Forest is felled, domestic stock are released to graze, new roads give quicker access to once-remote places and firearms make the killing of deer easier. This is not the place to catalogue all the sorry tales of the demise of deer but a few examples will be mentioned.

South America: all the native deer of South America are at risk. Of these, the delightful little pudu is the only one to be seen in any British zoos. Its surviving wild populations are reduced to a few localities in the lower ranges of the Andes. The red and brown brockets, marsh deer, the largest deer on this continent, and two species of huemal are all now threatened. Named after its flat, open grassland habitat, which formerly extended for hundreds of thousands of square miles, the pampas deer was once the dominant plant-eating mammal. Last century millions were killed for various purposes but especially for the export trade in their beautiful skins. Now it is one of the rarest deer, being reduced to a few small remnant populations in Argentina, Paraguay, Uraguay, Brazil and Bolivia. Its habitat has been altered and there is feeding competition from the large herds of ranched cattle and from numerous brown hares, an alien species introduced from Europe.

Pampas deer, after the original design by Alfred Waterhouse for the Natural History Museum.

Asia: the picture is no rosier in Asia. Here, also, many as yet little-known deer face one or more of the usual man-imposed threats. One of these is the white-lipped deer, also known as the white-faced Tibetan, Przewalskii or Thorold's deer. It lives at high altitudes on the Tibetan Plateau where its populations have been depleted by hunting as well as a tremendous increase in the number of domestic yaks and sheep sharing its alpine meadows.

The Manipur brow-antlered deer *(Cervus eldi eldi)* is on the verge of extinction. Although the remaining deer (less than one hundred in 1990) are within the Keibul Lamjao National Park, there is illegal encroachment by cattle and buffaloes belonging to unsympathetic local people. The main feeding habitat of the deer consists of rafts of floating humus and vegetation known as phumdi, which may be 2 metres (6.5 ft) thick. The deer splay the cleaves of their feet to spread their weight when on this quaking surface. A mat 80 cm (30 in) deep is said to support the weight of a stag weighing about 100 kg (220 lb). The plight of this deer is but one illustration of the need to consider the socio-economic factors of local communities when planning conservation strategies.

The Formosan sika deer became extinct in the wild on Taiwan (formerly Formosa) in 1969 but a few years ago a reintroduction project was begun. Stock from Taipei Zoo was released, initially within enclosures, in a newly designated National Park in the south of the island. The island's own sub-species of sambar deer is vulnerable and one wonders how long the Formosan muntjac populations can survive the hunting pressure which has increased enormously in the last decade.

Perhaps the world's most endangered deer is Prince Alfred's, also known as the Philippine spotted deer. Endemic to the central Philippines, it is extinct on all but two little islands where very small numbers have a tenuous hold. Forest clearance to make temporary agricultural plots and commercial felling have reduced the rain forest to small isolated patches and created severe soil erosion. A captive breeding project was begun in 1982 but five years later five of the precious few deer were lost during a raid by a guerilla army.

In south-west Iran an extremely small number, perhaps a handful, of Mesopotamian fallow survive in a narrow strip of riverine scrub and woodland. A captive herd is maintained in a wooded park near the Caspian Sea and a few originating from there are present on two islands. Another park in Iran and the Hai-Bar Reserve in Israel also have some Mesopotamian fallow but their stock came from German zoos where, in the past, their forebears may have been crossed with European fallow, so their genetic purity may not be one hundred per cent. The total of Mesopotamian fallow in Iran in 1990 was under two hundred. Some German zoos have also supplied deer farmers in New Zealand who wish to obtain a larger carcase by hybridizing them with European fallow. The first generation cross gave body weights, by one year of age, twenty per cent heavier than the European fallow on the same farm.

Ups as well as downs

In contrast to these few examples of declining species, the populations of moose in Norway, Sweden and Poland have risen dramatically in the last few decades. Over much of Europe roe and red deer have also increased, both in range and numbers, but several sub-species of red deer are severely endangered. These include the Corsican, which is extinct in the wild on Corsica but of which a few hundred survive on Sardinia. Conservation efforts have saved the Bactrian red deer from extinction in Russia where it inhabits a very hot, arid region but it is, at best, very rare in Afghanistan. The Kashmir red deer populations, estimated at under a thousand, have declined because of poaching. Virtually nothing is known of the Tibetan red deer ('shou') which was re-discovered, in Bhutan, in 1982, nearly sixty years after its suspected extinction! MacNeill's deer remains in just one province, Sichuan, of China on the border with Tibet but some are farmed for their antler velvet.

The Barbary red deer has the distinction of being the only native deer in Africa, although fallow have been introduced to South Africa. Some two

From China and back

The best known story of deer conservation is that of the 'milu' or Père David deer of China. When some of these animals were first seen within the Imperial Hunting Park in 1865 by the Basque missionary, naturalist and explorer whose name they bear, they were already extinct in the wild. Their history as a park animal was long and their fossil record shows that formerly they were distributed widely in eastern China.

In what was perhaps the first concerted effort to save a mammal from extinction, early this century the Duke of Bedford gathered together all eighteen available specimens of milu from zoos in Europe to create one herd at Woburn Park in Bedfordshire. (The last few milu in China met unfortunate ends about this time.) From this small nucleus herd there are now about 1,500 distributed in parks and zoos around the world. Fortunately there is no apparent genetic impairment from inbreeding. The story came full circle in 1985 and 1986 when two consignments, of 22 and 39 milu, were flown from England to China to establish two enclosed herds. One is on the site where Père David first saw the species. Both reserves include swampy reed beds and open water for which the deer show preference.

Milu are certainly very distinctive. Their tail is the longest

Milu at rutting time.

of all the deer and, as one of their native names implies, they look a mixture of a horse, a cow and a goat as well as a deer. The antlers lack brow tines and appear to be put on back-to-front; they make very good hay-racks in the rut (July-August) when the deer be-deck them with vegetation, a habit

shared with several species of deer, presumably to make their super-structure look even more impressive to rivals or to females. Milu grow their antlers during the winter and shed the velvet in spring, about the time that the females are calving.

thousand Barbary deer now live on each side of the Tunisian/Algerian border, a spectacular rise since thirty years ago when only ten survived in Tunisia and an unknown number in Algeria. This increase is attributed to the establishment of a 40,000-acre (16,000-hectare) forest reserve and the control of poaching.

In North America wapiti and white-tailed deer have also increased. The latter are the most abundant and widespread species on that continent. Their range spans 70° latitude, from southern Canada to southern Peru, the longest natural north-south distribution of any deer. This distance includes a diverse range of habitats and within the 38 sub-species described there is a wide range in body size. The most northerly are a little taller than fallow deer but they diminish southwards. The smallest of these, the Florida Key deer, is shorter than a roe deer, and this sub-species is threatened by loss of habitat.

White-tailed buck.

Fossil forms

Our knowledge of the evolution of the deer family is sketchy. We believe that in the Late Oligocene, some 30 million years ago, small forest-dwelling animals, somewhat like the chevrotains of today, gave rise to the families we know as musk deer, deer, cattle and antelopes, giraffes and pronghorns. By the Early Miocene there were in Europe a range of cud-chewing mammals with bony out-growths on the head. Most of these structures were horns but the earliest true, antler-shedding deer appears in Middle Miocene deposits in Europe. Called *Dicroceros*, it had simple forked antlers and was of small body size; it occurred from 21 million until 3 million years ago. The present-day tufted deer and the muntjacs may be descended from a form very similar to *Dicroceros*. Later in the Miocene there is evidence of some deer with flattened rounded ends to their antlers.

GEOLOGICAL PERIODS RELEVANT TO THE EVOLUTION OF DEER

Epoch	Approx. duration in millions of years
Holocene (Recent)	0.01
Pleistocene	1.9
Pliocene	3
Miocene	19
Oligocene	12

The Pliocene was the epoch during which the various types of deer multiplied in the forested parts of Eurasia. Fossil forms related to roe, red, moose, axis and rusa, as well as muntjac, can be recognized. The earliest antlered animals known in North America date from this period, having entered from Eurasia. Here too they continued to evolve. Upper Pliocene deposits have yielded specimens of an antlered genus, *Parablastomeryx*. The formation of a land bridge between North America and South America during this epoch enabled many species of animals to spread from the north, so by the Pleistocene both of these continents had various types of deer.

The divergence of species adapted to different habitats and diets accelerated in the Pleistocene. In Britain the deer of this period are especially well represented among the faunal remains of the north

Norfolk coast. Norwich Castle Museum has a fine collection of these specimens, and stormy seas continue to dislodge more examples from their ancient resting places. The Weybourn Crag, formed during the Lower Pleistocene, is exposed on the foreshore. From this crag come two genera of deer, *Eucladoceros* (formerly called *Euctenoceros*) and *Cervalces* (the ancestor of present-day moose and formerly called *Libralces*). Both became extinct before modern times. One of them, *Eucladoceros sedgwicki*, had at least eight points on each antler and has been called the comb- or bush-antlered deer. The higher, younger strata exposed on the Norfolk cliffs, known as the Upper Freshwater Bed, date from the Cromerian Interglacial period. The deer identified here include several species of *Megaloceros*, including *M. verticornis* which later became extinct, roe, red deer and also Clacton fallow deer, *Dama dama clactoniana*.

The most complete skull and antlers of Clacton fallow, which can be seen at the Natural History Museum in London, was found in Hoxnian Interglacial deposits at Swanscombe, Kent, but the first, fragmentary finds were from the Essex coastal town whose name the fossil bears. The species has been found in many other localities in Britain and continental Europe. The Clacton fallow was a fifth to a third larger than our present-day fallow with splendid palmed antlers. By the Last Interglacial fallow deer had become smaller. Leg bones found in Devon and in many European countries indicate that they were intermediate between those of Clacton and modern fallow. After this time fallow disappear from the fossil record in Britain. Evidently they died out here during the Last Glaciation and when later the climate improved they failed to re-colonize Britain before it became an island.

The giant deer of the genus *Megaloceros* are of particular interest. The best known species was *Megaloceros* (formerly called *Megoceros*) *giganteus* which existed in the Middle to late Upper Pleistocene. It has been called the Irish elk but it wasn't an elk and, although the finest and greatest number of specimens have been found in Ireland, it occurred in the grassland areas over much of Eurasia. Great Britain and Ireland were still joined to the continent when the giant deer appeared in Ireland in the middle part of the last glaciation. Abrupt climatic changes caused other alterations in the environment which led to its extinction, along with mammoths and woolly rhinoceroses, around 10,000 years ago. Nevertheless we know much about the giant deer because whole skeletons have been found and some Upper Palaeolithic (Old Stone Age) people left remarkably good drawings on their cave walls. A male deer was about

peat

gravel

peat

clay

shell marl

clay

Probing an Irish peat bog for remains of Megaloceros *(after J. G. Millais).*

1.8 metres (6 ft) tall at the shoulder and looked like a giant fallow deer. Examination of the skeleton provides clues to its life-style, such as its ability to run speedily over flat terrain. The fragments of willow found on the teeth of one specimen support other evidence indicating that they lived on low-lying lake shores and river valleys.

Very few remains of female giant deer have been found. This could be because for much of the year the sexes were segregated, as fallow and red deer are in the present time, and only male-occupied localities have been discovered to date. Alternatively the method of finding the skeletons may have been biased in favour of the number of males found. When searching of the Irish peat bogs was in its hey-day a century ago, the usual technique was for a man to push a very long iron pole through the peat to the underlying clay. If the pole hit something hard at several places within a few feet, then digging began. An antler, being larger than a limb, is more likely to be struck. Sometimes a cast antler had been struck but frequently the antler was still attached to the skull. Some antlers were over 2 metres

THE PLEISTOCENE EPOCH IN BRITAIN

Sub-division	Culture	Approx. yrs B.P.	Climate	Deer in Britain
	Neolithic	5,000	Present Interglacial	Red Roe
	Mesolithic	10,000		
UPPER	Upper Palaeolithic	30,000	Last (Devensian) Cold Stage	Red Reindeer
	Middle Palaeolithic	100,000		Moose *M. giganteus**
		120,000	Last (Ipswichian) Interglacial	Red Roe Fallow *M. giganteus**
			Penultimate (Wolstonian) Cold Stage	Red Reindeer *M. giganteus**
		200,000	_ _ _ _ _ _ _ _ _ _	
		300,000	Hoxnian Interglacial	Red Roe Clacton fallow *M. giganteus**
	Lower Palaeolithic		Anglian Cold Stage _ _ _ _ _ _ _ _ _ _	Red Reindeer *M.** species
MIDDLE			Cromerian Interglacial	Red Roe Fallow species *M. verticornis** *M. savini** *Cervalces latifrons**
		700,000	_ _ _ _ _ _ _ _ _ _ _ _ _ _ _ _ _ _ _ _	
LOWER			alternation of many cool and warm stages	*Eucladoceros* species* early *Cervus* species* *Cervalces gallicus**
		2,000,000		

* = became extinct   M. = *Megaloceros*   _ _ _ = various interglacials as yet un-named
Red = *Cervus elaphus*   Roe = *Capreolus capreolus*   Moose = *Alces alces*
Fallow = *Dama dama dama*

(7 ft.) long with a very broad palm of about 60 cm. (2 ft.). Mounted whole skeletons can be seen in a number of museums. Careful observation of them may reveal two left shin bones, lower leg bones of unequal size or other errors! Such discrepancies result from the method of storing piles of

excavated bones before dispatching a set of them as a DIY assembly kit to the purchasing museum.

Elsewhere in the world during the Pleistocene many more of the present-day deer were becoming established, including *Axis* in Java and Père David deer in China and Japan. Moose *(Libralces)* are known in Eurasia from the Early Pleistocene onwards and reindeer *(Rangifer)* from the Middle Pleistocene. Both of these reached America much later.

As more fossils come to light and palaeontologists re-appraise those already found, the picture of deer evolution will gradually become clearer. There are many problems in working with incomplete material. Although antlers can be very useful in suggesting possible relationships among deer, they must be used with caution. One must consider the variation possible in size and form among antlers from males of the same age from one locality or in one individual at different years of his life. Similarly, comparing the sizes of bones from different geological periods may not be sound unless one knows the sex of the animals, for male deer are usually larger than females.

Buck or stag, doe or hind?

The history of man's association with deer of various species is long and fascinating and with this grew a rich vocabulary of specialized terms. Many of them have fallen into disuse but a few of those still used are listed here.

Species	*Male/female/young*
Red, sika	Stag/hind/calf
Fallow, muntjac, Chinese water deer	Buck/doe/fawn
Roe	Buck/doe/kid
Reindeer	Bull/cow/calf

Beam:	the main stem of an antler	Pricket:	a fallow with his first antlers
Cull:	to shoot surplus deer	Slots:	footprints of a deer
Gralloch:	stomach and intestines of a deer	Tine:	point on an antler
Head:	a pair of antlers e.g. first head/ a good head		

Sex symbols: ♂ male: ♀ female

Who's who in Britain

RED DEER *(Cervus elaphus scoticus)*
Ever since 'Monarch of the Glen' was painted in 1851, and subsequently reproduced for Victorian homes throughout the land, people have considered a red stag as a majestic beast, even if nowadays they see the picture only as a small reproduction on a bottle of whisky. The whole demeanour of a red deer, stag or hind, its gaze, stance and gait, give the impression of a haughty, superior being and such anthropomorphic feelings are conveyed in Landseer's painting. The royal connotations are reinforced by the term 'a royal' for a stag with twelve points (all 'his rights') of which three on each antler form a 'crown' ('cup') large enough to hold a wine glass.

The first pair of antlers are single spikes (with exceptions in some captive situations) but later heads produce tines off the main beam. Just

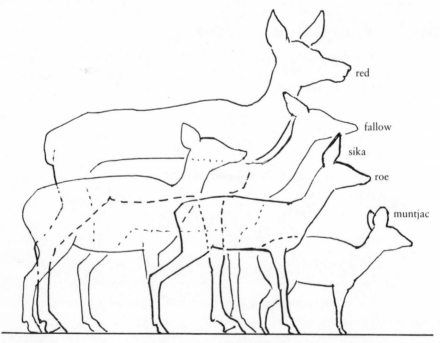

red
fallow
sika
roe
muntjac

Comparative sizes of female deer.

Young red deer stag in winter coat.

above the base (coronet) of the antler is the brow tine. Further up is the 'bez' (pronounced and sometimes spelt bay) and higher still is the 'trez' (tray) tine. The antler terminates in a single point, or cluster of points ('cup'). One cannot tell the age of a deer from the number of points he carries but the form and size of the antlers give an indication of whether he is young, middle-aged or elderly. Other factors that must be taken into account include where that population of deer is living, body size and condition.

The red deer's name refers to its rich red-brown summer coat on which some individuals have a scattering of slightly paler spots. The winter coat is dull brown and at this time the males have a mane of longer, coarser hairs on the neck. The rump is buff and the tail is held close to it.

White red deer occur rarely in the wild: often in legend and literature they have been regarded as an omen. White herds have been kept in a few parks in Britain and other European countries, the best known being the Zehucice Deer Park in Central Bohemia, Czechoslovakia, where many deer are white, some are normal red colour and others are parti-coloured. White parents may have calves of any of these varieties. Many of the white deer have a small patch of red somewhere on the body which makes

cup (crown)

trez

bez

brow

Twelve pointer ('royal') red deer stag.

individual recognition possible without tagging them and has enabled detailed behavioural studies to be made of this herd.

Red deer occur right across Europe, parts of Asia and just into North Africa while their larger cousins, the wapiti, extend over much of Asia and North America. Consequently our native red deer has twenty close relations all now regarded as sub-species of *Cervus elaphus*. The British *C. e. scoticus* is amongst the smallest of them all. Outwardly they differ from each other in antler form and size as well as body size and colour, especially of the rump patch, tail and any markings along the back. There are also variations in voice and behaviour and adaptations to different habitats and climates.

Whereas sub-species geographically near to each other differ only slightly, when the sub-species at the two ends of the range are compared the differences are much greater. If comparison is made between those at the extremities of the range, without taking into account those on the way, then it can be hard even to see a relationship. Such a gradual change in any species over a band of latitude or longitude is known as a 'cline', but the variation among different populations of the same sub-species must be borne in mind. For example, the Scottish red deer resident in forests attain

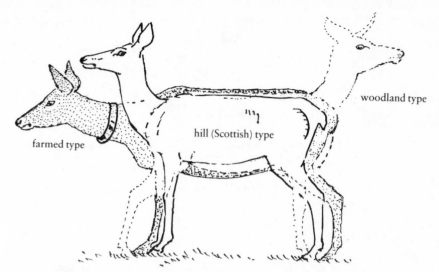

Red deer living in Scottish forests are larger than those resident on the open hill.

greater size than those living on exposed moorland habitats not far away. Similarly Norwegian red deer, *C. e. atlanticus*, are heavier in the north of their range than in the south and those inland are heavier than those near the coast, differences believed to be associated with the quality of the herbage. The natural distribution of the Central European red deer (*C. e. hippelaphus*) spans many countries from France to western Russia and, by introduction, it also occurs in Chile and Argentina. The antlers have more points than any of the other red deer.

The behaviour and performance of the woodland red deer and those of the open habitats differ in many respects. Much information has come from studies of red deer on the wet, exposed Hebridean island of Rhum, where a team of biologists has been observing them for nearly two decades. The years of recording data collected during observations on individually known animals and its subsequent analysis and interpretation have yielded a huge body of information on the ecology and reproductive performance of this population which has been presented in the book *Red Deer; Behavior and Ecology of Two Sexes*. Other studies have been done on mainland Scotland (partly stimulated by the impact of deer on timber crops and their influence on the natural regeneration of ancient Caledonian pine forest). About three-quarters of mainland Scotland is tree-less moorland and mountain and red deer occupy about half of this area. In contrast, other red deer populations are resident within forests which

Hinds fighting

J □

Hard times in Highlands: seek food and shelter in low ground.

Food scarce.

F □■ begins 16th

Hard times in Highlands.

Feed in fields if can.

M □■●

Antlers cast, old stags first.

A □■●

Moult: bleached coats.

Calving begins.

M □■○●

Red summer coats.

Males in velvet.

Calving continues.

J □■○●

Stags boxing.

Calves lose spots.

J ○●■

Cleaning antlers.

A ●■

Stags split up: solitary or with hinds. Rut begins late Sept.

S ●■

Rut continues.

O □ begins 21st ■ ends 20th ●

Mature stags exhausted.

N □

Stag parties and hind herds.

D □

CLOSE SEASONS KEY	♂	♀
England & Wales	○	●
Scotland	□	■

The red deer year.

provide better year-round shelter and food. Results show that the woodland hinds first calve at the age of two years, as they do in English parks, and thereafter breed every year. Hinds on Rhum and other open localities do not calve until three or more years old, then alternate barren and breeding years. Furthermore, their calf mortality is three times as high as it is for the woodland deer. Consequently the forest populations have a greater potential to increase rapidly, and in a situation where control is more difficult.

The New Zealand experience

Australia and New Zealand lack any endemic deer but settlers soon introduced an assortment of deer from other continents. In New Zealand over 230 liberations of red deer from Britain, involving at least 850 animals, took place during a 70-year period commencing about 1851. In the absence of any native mammals, the red deer exploited the vast food-rich areas of mountain forests and lowland pastures so numbers increased at a tremendous rate. By 1930 a control campaign was initiated and within four years 100,000 deer had been shot. This was only the beginning of a difficult battle the various phases of which have been reviewed in The Deer Wars. Two decades later the annual cull was 50,000 and a venison export trade had been created, but many shot deer were left to rot because of the inaccessibility by vehicle of the terrain. This led to the cullers operating from helicopters so that freshly shot carcases could be hoisted off the mountains. In just one year one 'chopper' crew alone killed 12,000 red deer. This hazardous work became very lucrative and the deer populations declined, leaving the future of the well established venison market insecure.

This circumstance led to the creation of the deer farming industry which flourishes today. Helicopter crews switched to netting live deer to provide breeding stock: a decade ago eighty crews were engaged in this dangerous operation. Now New Zealand is regarded as the deer farming centre of the world.

SIKA DEER *(Cervus nippon)*

Sika were the first of the Asiatic deer to be imported to the British Isles. Between 1860 and 1930 sika were introduced to about 6 locations in Ireland, 13 in Scotland, 40 in England and 2 in Wales. Most of the introductions were to parks and escapes from some subsequently occurred. The feral sika here today are generally regarded as Japanese *(Cervus nippon nippon)*, although some of the parks did at one time also have Manchurian or Formosan sika. These are the three main types although up to thirteen sub-species have been described.

The summer coat of the Japanese sika is similar to that of a common coloured fallow deer but the black line down the tail is narrower and often shorter or absent. This spotted chestnut-brown coat is moulted in autumn and replaced by a very dark, almost black, winter one. In this coat they look a bit like a black fallow, but the sika are more uniformly dark. The ears of the sika are more rounded than those of fallow. Any possible confusion with fallow, which are only marginally larger, will be dispelled if the frightened sika runs away, flaring the hairs of its prominent white rump patch.

A stag has a slightly paler marking on the forehead, just above the eyes, which gives him an angry, scowling appearance which seems accentuated when he develops a mane in autumn. The maximum number of points on each antler of a mature stag is four. The first pair are single spikes but the second set may have two, three or four tines. Like red deer and other members of the genus *Cervus*, sika have a small black patch on the lower lip just in front of the corner of the mouth.

Sika deer in winter coat (on left) *and summer coat* (on right).

Sika hinds (left) *and fallow does* (right) *in summer.*

In recent years interest in sika has centred on their hybridization with red deer which has occurred in several areas, causing concern for the future genetic purity of the native red deer. In Co. Wicklow and the English Lake District whole populations appear to be hybrids rather than pure-bred red or sika. Hybrids have also been reported from Argyllshire, Sutherland and Inverness-shire. Further instances are likely as the sika continue to extend their range within Scottish habitats already occupied by the native red deer. A few years ago they were advancing into new areas of Argyllshire at the rate of 2-3 miles (3-5 km) a year.

Observations on sika in Dorset indicated that during the day they remained within the coniferous forest, emerging from cover to feed on the adjacent fields at night. Yet a short distance away, in the adjacent county of Hampshire, the sika of the New Forest were likely to be active at any time and, having a wider choice of habitats, for much of the year about half their time was spent in deciduous woodland. Such variations in behaviour among different populations, which fit their life-styles to the local conditions of food availability and disturbance, occur in other deer species too.

FALLOW DEER *(Dama dama)*

The fallow is considered by many to be the most pleasing of our deer, in appearance and taste! Both were good reasons for keeping them in deer parks, often on their own, sometimes with red deer and, occasionally, within the last century, with sika deer.

One of their attractions is the range of colours within the species. No other deer comes in so many different colours although reindeer show considerable variation. The main colour varieties are common, menil, black and white. Some park owners prefer to maintain a herd of just one colour while others like a mixture. Wild populations include all these colours although there is local variation as to which predominates.

In summer the common coloured fallow is rich brown with white spots, changing to dull greyish brown with indistinct or no spots in winter. The menil type is a paler version of the common colour and retains some spots in winter. They have a brown line along the middle of the back, down the tail and round the rump whereas all these markings are black on the common coloured deer.

White fallow have no dark markings. They are pale ginger when born but become creamier with the first few moults. Their hooves are pale, instead of boot-polish black but their eyes are normal so they are only partial albinos. The black fallow has a glossy jet coat in summer on which there are indistinct paler, browner spots. In winter the coat is sooty, with the upper half darker than the lower parts of the flanks and belly. All these colour varieties can interbreed and the offspring are sometimes different from either parent. For example, one captive black doe mated by a menil

A common-coloured fallow doe shows her rump and tail markings as she grooms.

Long-haired fallow doe and fawn in Mortimer Forest.

buck had a common coloured fawn.

There is another type of variation in the coat of fallow deer but it has only been reported from one area, in and around Mortimer Forest in Shropshire. Here there are a number of long-haired fallow. The body hairs are about three times the usual length and are more noticeable on the winter coat. Even more eye-catching are the long curly hairs on the forehead and others that flow from the ears.

The antlers of a fallow buck are very distinctive. Apart from moose, no other living deer have broad, flattened palms, but these are not attained until the buck is several years old. The first antlers are simple spikes or less elegant dumpy knobs. Exceptionally a wild fallow produces one or two tines off the beam of his first antlers. Proof of this came with observations and photographs of an Essex fallow which had been ear-tagged as a newly born fawn, and it may be more common than hitherto reported.

The second and subsequent antlers have a brow and a trez tine but lack the bez tine that is present on red stags. Slight palmation is often seen on the second set of antlers, but sometimes not until the third or fourth set.

Even the best fallow antlers in Britain are seldom up to the standard commonly found in some other countries. Hungary is especially famous for its beautifully antlered and heavy-bodied bucks.

In southern England fallow may shed their antlers as early as the end of March but May and June are more likely. Older males cast earlier, needing longer in which to grow larger antlers, but most will be fully grown and clean by the end of August or early September. Some fallow antlers, particularly second and third heads, have incomplete, porous tips. This occurs when the antler hasn't been completely mineralized into hard bone by the time the velvet is shed, so the soft tip breaks and falls off with the velvet.

Just as the Normans brought fallow to Britain in the medieval period, centuries later emigrants transported them around the world. Fallow from England, or in some instances another European country, were shipped to destinations as diverse as Australia, New Zealand, Argentina, Chile, one Fijian island, Barbuda in the West Indies, islands east of Vancouver Island and the USA. They are now present as free-ranging populations in thirty-eight countries, where they have adapted to various habitats but in Britain prefer areas with a mosaic of deciduous or mixed woodland and pastures.

The fallow so far referred to is the European fallow. Its closest relation is the Mesopotamian fallow. This is larger but otherwise very similar in appearance to a common coloured European fallow. The main distinction is the form of the antlers. The Mesopotamians lack the broad palm although typically have some flattening at the upper end and rather more at the lower end of the beam. The brow tine is very short. The plight of this sub-species is mentioned on page 12.

Magpies on fallow does in a deer park.

ROE DEER *(Capreolus capreolus)*

Like the red deer, roe have been present in Britain for hundreds of thousands of years. Our roe is *Capreolus capreolus* whose distribution extends across most of Europe, into Turkey, parts of the Middle East and central Russia. The larger Siberian (Asian) roe occurs in eastern Russia, Mongolia, China and Korea. Because of the severity of the winters there, some roe populations in Russia migrate for about 200 miles (300 km.) to areas where the snow will not become too deep.

A startled six-pointer roe buck.

In winter roe have wonderfully thick coats of bristly almost erect hairs which are predominantly grey flecked with beige, except for a white rump patch. In May-June this coat is shed gradually, a process during which the deer looks moth-eaten and tatty until the beautiful foxy-red summer coat of shorter, sleeker hairs is completely grown. The rump patch is now cream and less conspicuous until the deer flairs these hairs as an alarm signal to other roe. The brush-like tuft of hairs that hangs from below the anus of a doe is not a tail, for the tail of a roe is seldom visible, being only a tiny stump buried within the hairs of the rump.

Some roe have two white patches, one at the throat, the other part way

Roe does in winter coat (left) *and summer coat* (right).

down the neck; but in some populations, such as those of the Breckland forests, they are absent or at most indistinct. Not only is the skin of the nose black, but also the adjacent patch of hairs, which extend to the corner of the mouth on the lower lip. These black markings usually contrast sharply with the white on the chin but that varies in extent.

A normal roe buck antler has a maximum of three points. The rapier-like tips make roe difficult deer to keep in captivity where they can become very aggressive and dangerous. This is one of the reasons why this species is seldom kept in zoos or parks. Typically the lower part of the antler is

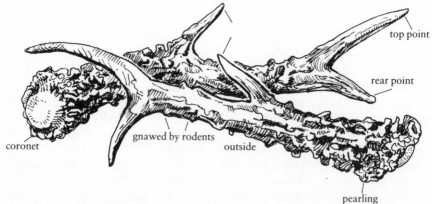

Two views of a cast right antler of a roe buck. The outer side has been gnawed by rodents while it lay on the ground. (Actual length c. 20 cm./8 in.).

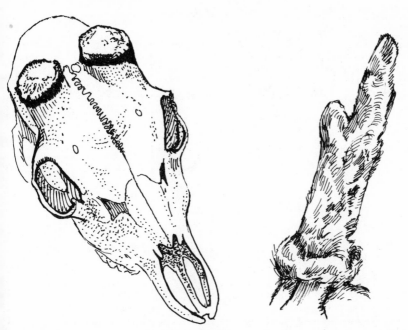

(Left) *Skull of a roe buck which died in December, just after he had cast his antlers. (Actual length of skull 19 cm./7.5 in.).* (Right) *The dense, furry velvet on the antler of a roe buck. (Actual length 21 cm./8.5 in.).*

much roughened by many little projections of the antler bone, collectively known as 'pearling'. The pedicles (see p.49) are close together so the coronet at the base of each antler virtually touches its partner, whereas in the other deer there is some expanse of forehead between the two. While growing, the antlers are covered in a much furrier velvet than on any of our other deer, probably because they are grown over the winter and need better insulation from the cold.

Although a few populations of roe live on moorland, their typical habitat is woodland with some thick cover, near grassy glades or fields. During the fifty or so years required for a timber crop to grow in commercial coniferous forests the ground and shrub layers of vegetation undergo changes, consequently their suitability for roe varies. A greater number of roe will occupy a plantation during the thicket-stage, when the trees are 3-10 m. (10-30 ft.) tall and it provides both plenty of food and adequate shelter.

In contrast to these woodland dwellers there are in parts of Europe

Males in velvet.

J ○□

Males in velvet.
Family groups.

F ○□

Several groups may feed together.
Males in velvet.

M ○●□

Males fraying to clean velvet. Begin moult.

A ●□ ■

Males clean. Kids born. Moult progresses.

M ●■

Males mark territory. Summer coats.

J ●■

Kids lose spots. Males bark. Chases. Rut begins.

HoH BoH

J ●■

Rut continues. Does piping.

A ●■

Kids like mini-adults. Adult males elusive.

S ●■

Winter coats. Browsing.

O ●□ begins 21st ■ ends 20th

Antler casting begins.

N ○□

Antlers cast.
Family parties.

D ○□

CLOSE SEASONS KEY	♂	♀
England & Wales	○	●
Scotland	□	■

The roe deer year.

populations known as field roe. They live in the open, finding small patches of trees or shrubs for shelter. Scores may be seen in one field, but it seems that they are not one cohesive herd but many small groups. Good forage is available in and around the arable fields for much of the year and in the early months food such as sugar beet roots left behind after harvesting can become the major item of diet, especially if snow persists. A snow depth of about 60 cm. (2 ft.) limits movements of roe as well as preventing access to herbage.

CHINESE WATER DEER *(Hydropotes inermis)*
The natural distribution of water deer is eastern China and Korea, with a different sub-species in each of those countries. It was the Chinese form, *Hydropotes inermis inermis*, which was imported to Woburn Park, Bedfordshire, early this century. In the 1930s some of their progeny were taken to Whipsnade Wild Animal Park which is still a good place to observe these delightful deer. Here they free-range within the extensive park, foraging on the slopes of the Dunstable Downs, moving in and out of paddocks and utilizing the farm field within the park. They are remarkably well concealed when they crouch in long grass but there is a good chance of observing their distinctive movement used when they spring up and flee at high speed, flinging out their hind legs in the manner of a hare. Looking for them in the wild, in the vicinity of Woodwalton Fen and particularly in the reed beds of the Norfolk Broads requires much greater patience and effort, but is all the more rewarding when one succeeds. They look more at home in these surroundings which resemble their native habitats of reeds and long grasses close to rivers and lakes.

The water deer are smaller than roe but they share a number of similarities such as reddish coats in summer, furry ears and black noses.

Chinese water deer bucks, winter (left) *and summer* (right).

The tusks of a Chinese water deer buck are formidable weapons.

The winter coat is composed of light sandy-grey hairs, even longer (42 mm./ 1¾ in.) than those of a roe, so deep that one can bury one's fingers in the pile. Water deer have a short, inconspicuous tail which is held close to the rump but it is always more visible than that of a roe. The lack of a white rump is a further distinction.

The most striking feature of this species is the tusks of the males which enable recognition of the sexes at a distance, despite the lack of antlers. In the females these upper canine teeth aren't very long; only about 1 cm. (½ in.) protrudes below the upper lip. In contrast, an adult buck's tusks are curved downwards and backwards, with about 7 cm. (nearly 3 in.) exposed. The whole tusk, seen only if the tooth is extracted from a skull, is more like 10 cm. (4½ in.). The back of the tusk has a sharp cutting edge. The efficiency of these weapons is further enhanced by their mobility within the tooth socket. Facial muscles control a band of movable gum round each of the tusks. They can be moved slightly so they don't get in the way while the buck grazes or hinged forwards, ready to strike a rival male. Presumably the bucks also use them in defence against predators.

MUNTJAC *(Muntiacus reevesi)*
The muntjac in Britain suffered an identity crisis until the early 1980s. Various authors described them, our smallest feral deer, as being Chinese muntjac, Indian muntjac, both species or hybrids of the two. The confusion arose because first Indian muntjac and later Chinese muntjac were introduced to Woburn. The alleged tendency of the Indian deer to attack dogs prompted the plan to shoot the lot and replace them with the smaller Chinese muntjac. The likelihood is that a few of the Indian species survived for a while early this century but it is the Chinese that is now so widely distributed in England.

A muntjac doe encounters a hare and a grey partridge during a sortie into a field.

This deer is more aptly called Reeves' muntjac *(Muntiacus reevesi reevesi)*, after an inspector of tea who named several animals in China, because, in that vast country, there are other species of muntjac, including the Indian. The latter is sometimes called the red muntjac and throughout its range (Nepal, SW China, India, Sri Lanka, across and down through the islands as far as Java and Borneo) there are many sub-species, nine being the currently accepted number.

All six species of muntjac are from SE Asia. They are small forest-dwellers. Various features show that they and the tufted deer are the most primitive members of the deer family. They differ from other deer in the way that each of the pedicles, which are very long, is a continuation of a ridge on the skull above each eye. Mainly because of these and their tusk-like teeth, it has been suggested that they should be placed in a separate family. The natural distribution of Reeves' muntjac is in sub-tropical forested areas of southern China. A slightly different sub-species, *M. r. micrurus*, lives in thick forests on Taiwan. In these countries vast numbers of muntjac are snared every year, for food and skins.

The summer coat of Reeves' muntjac is a glossy rich, red-brown with a golden nape and face. In autumn the moult to the darker brown winter coat is almost imperceptible whereas the reverse moult in the spring is, as in most deer, a much more conspicuous and scruffy-looking process. The front of the fore-legs is often very dark, almost black, in the winter, especially on adult males. The belly is buff. The inside of the thighs is white, and so is the underside of the tail, the most conspicuous feature when a frightened deer runs away. Although muntjac often stand with their backs hunched, just as often they will be seen with straight backs.

The head markings differ in the two sexes. Adult males have a V of black lines on the forehead which extends up the pedicles but the females have a dark kite-shaped marking of which the outer edges are the blackest part. In both sexes the ears have a white edge but on the back they vary from almost black to golden: the inside is sparsely haired. The white chin is seldom conspicuous unless the deer raises its head to scent the air. Sometimes the very long tongue is rapidly extended as far as the sub-orbital area at the corner of the eye. On an adult buck the tusks can be seen in profile.

Following its introduction to southern England early this century the muntjac has become a well established member of our fauna. Its success can be attributed to a number of factors. Foremost among these must be

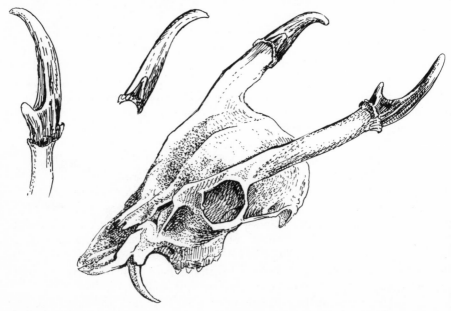

Skull of a muntjac buck showing an upper canine tooth, large sub-orbital pit, long pedicles and small antlers.

Bramble thickets provide excellent cover as well as food.

the potential for a female to produce a fawn every seven months. Fawns are born in any month of the year and within a day or two of giving birth a doe will usually conceive again. For the first half or more of the pregnancy she will be suckling a fawn while the next develops in her uterus. In addition to these physiological demands she may also be coping with harsh weather. In the occasional severe winters experienced in the southern half of England, when there is deep snow for a prolonged period, foraging becomes difficult. In the exceptionally hard winters of 1940 and 1953 many muntjac died. Given a normal winter they manage well, especially if they have fat reserves formed during an autumn when acorns and beech mast were abundant.

Muntjac don't require extensive woodland; small copses with plenty of cover and a selection of herbs and shrubs will suffice. Bramble thickets are especially good as they provide food for most of the year and excellent shelter. Undisturbed gardens are included within the home range of many muntjac and roses, ivy, honeysuckle, clematis, peas and beans are among the plants they select.

Not infrequently a muntjac will travel too far into a built-up area, creating a hazard for motorists as well as itself. Smashed French windows and an injured deer, or worse, are usually the outcome of these urban wanderings. More often than not the errant muntjac is a 'teenage' (sub-adult) male who has been pushed out of the area where he was born and, while dispersing, perhaps has been scared by dogs, people or traffic into taking a wrong direction.

Being small, secretive and mostly solitary, muntjac are inconspicuous

Proof of identification

Reeves' and red muntjac are distinct in colour and size. Although the English deer looked like Reeves', their appearance was not proof enough to rule out the possibility of their being hybrids. Two lines of investigation were pursued to establish finally which muntjac were at liberty in English woodlands.

Some of our large, long-established museums have skulls of muntjac brought back long ago by naturalists who visited India and China. A series of measurements were taken from all the available specimens and these separated into two distinct ranges of sizes for the two species. The same measurements were taken for over one hundred skulls of feral muntjac killed in England. These figures all fell within the ranges for the Reeves' skulls.

The second test involved investigation of the chromosomes, the structures in a cell that carry the genes which determine the inherited characters of an animal. Examination of the nuclei of some white blood cells and skin cells showed that the English muntjac had 46 chromosomes, the same as the Reeves' muntjac. This is a low number compared with other deer, most of which have 68-70.

However, the number in Reeves' very clearly distinguishes it from the Indian muntjac, which has the amazingly low number of 6 (female) and 7 (male). The basic explanation is that during evolution a larger number of small chromosomes have fused to form a small number of big ones. Incidentally, the possession of few, large chromosomes make Indian muntjac cells, cultured in a laboratory, suitable for investigating the effects of carcinogenic or other harmful substances and viruses on chromosomes.

The evidence of the chromosome number, the lengths and ratios of various skull bones as well as the physical appearance of the animal all showed that the muntjac in England was Reeves'. In captivity Indian and Reeves' muntjac have cross-bred which is surprising in view of the difference in chromosome number. As so often is the case with hybrids, the offspring were infertile. To have a population of hybrid muntjac the two species would have to be living together and continually inter-breeding, as well as breeding true to perpetuate the separate species. Clearly this is not the situation.

and can become established in an area before people are aware of their presence. On the whole they do little agricultural or silvicultural damage although certain broad-leaved trees and field crops or garden plants may be vulnerable in localized areas. Muntjac have fewer internal parasites than other deer and are usually very healthy.

REINDEER *(Rangifer tarandus)*
When Johnny Marks wrote 'Rudolph the red-nosed reindeer' he certainly knew how to write a perennially popular seasonal song, but he knew little of deer biology. Of all the deer the reindeer is the one with the least possibility of getting a red, shiny nose because there is no bare skin on the

A reindeer bull with a mane and good antlers.

nose, the whole area being covered by hair. This is just one of the reindeer's many adaptations for life in a cold, harsh environment, for they are the most northern member of the family.

The coat colour can be of many different shades of grey, off white, beige or brown. Some individuals, most often females and youngsters, have a series of lighter coloured spots or short vertical stripes along the flanks which have been called Pepper's patches after the artist who described them a few years ago. Earlier painters had depicted the markings on their cave paintings in France and Spain dating from 10,000-19,000 years ago. At that time reindeer distribution extended that far south and probably cave dwellers followed the migrations of the herds.

A reindeer's winter coat consists of a dense under-fur and thick, hollow outer hairs which together make a very efficient insulating layer, also acting as a buoyant life-jacket when the animal takes to the water. They swim fast with the body remaining remarkably high in the water so that the back and the tail, which is held vertically, are well clear of the surface. It is reported that reindeer do not sweat, even during strenuous exercise and little heat is lost through the fur.

Reindeer in Britain

There have been differences of opinion regarding the time at which reindeer died out in Britain. Recent reappraisal of all the available evidence put the date at around 8,000 years ago. They qualify for a chapter here because they were re-introduced to one locality in Scotland nearly forty years ago. Perhaps, too, I should admit to a special admiration for this animal. Although there is a vast amount of scientific literature on Scandinavian reindeer and North American caribou, with occasional symposia and a regular journal solely devoted to these deer, there is little readily available in English to give an insight into the lives of these northern wonders.

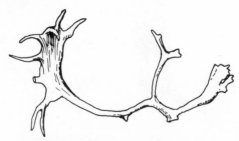

Cast antler, 122 cm./4 feet long, of a reindeer found in British Pleistocene deposits.

Visitors to the Highlands of Scotland have the opportunity to see reindeer south of Glenmore Forest Park, roaming the northern slopes of the Cairngorms between 400 and 1,300 metres. (1,300-4,225 ft.) Their forebears were imported from northern Sweden between 1952 and 1961. The herd is now maintained at about seventy animals. Since the arrival of the reindeer the area around Aviemore has been developed as a ski centre and holiday resort. There is a 1,000-acre (400 ha.) enclosure into which the animals are herded several times a year. Most births occur there, all through May and into June. The cows have their first calves around the time of their own second birthday. Most of the males are gelded, only a few entire bulls being kept for breeding.

While they are enclosed additional food, such as mixed cereals, is provided. Most of the year the reindeer free-range over the mountains. In the spring they enjoy the young grasses and birch shoots; in autumn they seek tasty toadstools but for most of the year their main food is lichens of which there are plenty on the mountains. In stormy, windy weather they usually move to higher elevations rather than down to the forest. Although snow is likely from September to May it is not deep until January.

Long-lasting, deep snow is to be expected in much of the natural range of reindeer. Their feet are not only broad, to spread their weight on snow or over boggy ground, but are also very hairy underneath, providing a non-slip sole. With the hooves they can dig down through snow for about 120 cm. (4 ft.) to find lichens and sedges. Only when thaw and re-freeze conditions occur, forming an impenetrable hard layer of ice, does foraging become impossible.

In the rest of the world
The present-day distribution of reindeer extends from Norway right across Eurasia to the east coast of Russia and in North America (where they are called caribou) they extend across Canada and Alaska. Some of the herds in Alaska are the descendants of thousands of reindeer brought from Siberia and Scandinavia at the end of the last century to replace the depleted populations of native caribou. The reports of the whole operation make fascinating reading. It entailed not only the purchase of the reindeer but also the hiring of herdsmen, who were to teach the husbandry to the Eskimos, and shipping them all, complete with sufficient fodder for the journey: one ship alone carried 500 tons of reindeer moss.

Introductions were also made to numerous islands including Greenland and Iceland. The latter, plus those on Svalbard and on South Georgia, are perhaps the luckiest of all reindeer as these islands lack the warbles, nasal bot flies, horse flies and mosquitoes which in most other places in summer torment reindeer. Blood-sucking insects may drain as much as 125 g. (5 oz.) of blood from one deer in a day. Much energy is expended in shaking or galloping to try to escape the attention of the flies. Resting in sandy places lessens their attacks slightly.

The reindeer populations on South Georgia are the result of introductions in 1911 and 1925. The stock, from Norway, was shipped to this sub-antarctic island as a source of sport and change of diet for Norwegians at the whaling station which functioned until 1965. The reindeer still thrive there. Their annual cycles of rutting, calving and antler growth are six months out of phase with reindeer in their native northern latitudes, having adapted to the seasons of the southern hemisphere as the fallow and red deer did when introduced to Australia and New Zealand.

Reindeer are migratory, some making relatively short seasonal altitudinal movements but other populations travelling over 600 miles (up to 1,000 km.) annually. About two hundred years ago the zoologist Pallas described the scene in NE Siberia when hundreds of thousands of reindeer on migration stretched across ten miles, their antlers looking like a moving forest. They leave the calving grounds near the Arctic Circle when the frosts begin and move southwards, following traditional routes each year, to forests where the snow will remain softer. When lengthening daylight heralds the spring, they begin the return trek, separate herds eventually coming together in hundreds or thousands.

Harnessing resources: the reindeer made it possible for humans to inhabit the inhospitable northern tundra, some tribes being dependent upon these animals for their entire economy. In Scandinavia and Russia various peoples domesticated the reindeer. A lasso was used to catch individual reindeer and ownership was indicated by ear-nicks of various patterns. Meat and milk, and therefore butter and cheese, pelts for clothes, boots, upholstery, bedding, tents and boats, tendons for stitching skins, antlers for utensils and even as a surface for artistic creativity — all can be obtained from reindeer. They are also good pack and draught animals: that part of the Santa Claus story rings true.

In Sweden there have not been any wild reindeer for over a hundred years but the present (1990) number of semi-domesticated stock is 300,000 (excluding this year's calves), with about 800 Lapp families more or less dependent on them. About 150,000 calves are born and around 100,000 reindeer are slaughtered annually. These figures would suggest a population increase each year of 50,000 but this is not so. There are heavy losses to starvation, diseases, predators and accidental deaths. The Chernobyl disaster continues to have a very severe impact on the reindeer industry; many of the winter pastures are heavily contaminated. Finland has a smaller stock of herded reindeer and a few hundred wild animals. In Norway, where reindeer herding dates back at least to the ninth century AD, the domesticated reindeer are mostly in the northern and middle two-thirds of the country. Some 35,000 wild reindeer occur in the alpine and sub-alpine birch forests of the southern third. Russia has the largest populations of wild and domesticated reindeer.

Hazards: although they live in remote and sparsely populated regions, reindeer are under increasing pressure from encroachment on their habitats by modern forestry, mining, urbanization, hydro-electric power installations, oil pipelines, roads, hikers, skiers, campers, snow-scooters, low-flying aircraft and airborne pollution. All of these can affect the behaviour of the herds, disrupt their normal patterns of feeding and movement or destroy their winter pastures. The females and calves are more readily disturbed than the bulls.

Sizing them up

Weights and measurements make dull reading, and most deer watchers need just an indication of the relative sizes of the different species. A muntjac is only (4 cm./ 1½ in.) less tall than a Labrador dog and a red stag's shoulder is about level with the waist of the average man; the other wild deer fit within these two ends of the scale. Those who want to know more can glance at the table on p.47, but they must remember that there can be a lot of variation between different populations.

For a landowner selling to a game-dealer the weights of the carcases are of economic importance. If a gradual decline is recorded in the mean weights of animals of the same sex and comparable age the likely explanation is that the land is over-stocked. Culling a higher than usual quota of deer should redress the balance, provided vegetation has not been seriously over-browsed or over-grazed. The carrying capacity of woodland, particularly conifer plantations, varies greatly during its life-time, a fact that must be borne in mind by managers of deer populations.

If weights of deer from different areas are to be compared the first essential is to ensure that like is compared with like. Are the available figures for the whole body, larder, butcher's or dressed weights? The first of these is rarely available for the larger deer. The gut (stomach plus intestines) can form a high proportion of the deer's total weight (e.g. twenty per cent or more in fallow) so it is customary to gralloch the animal when it is shot to reduce the weight to be carried back to the venison house. There has been a recent trend against this practice in some areas for reasons of hygiene. For the other categories of weights check exactly what is meant by the term on the estate concerned. Whether the head, feet and skin are on or off makes a big difference. Also check whether all internal organs have been removed.

Some stags appear to test the height of a fence: if the chin reaches the top, they can jump the fence.

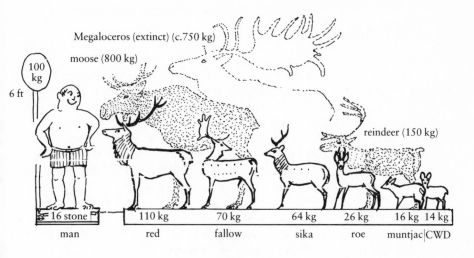

Megaloceros (extinct) (c.750 kg)

moose (800 kg)

reindeer (150 kg)

100 kg

6 ft

man	red	fallow	sika	roe	muntjac	CWD
16 stone	110 kg	70 kg	64 kg	26 kg	16 kg	14 kg

WEIGHTS AND HEIGHTS

Species	*Weight*	*Height at shoulder*
Red (Scotland)		
male	93-122 kg. (205-268 lb.)	122 cm. (48 in.)
female	68-90 kg. (150-198 lb.)	114 cm. (45 in.)
Fallow (Essex)		
male	46-80 kg. (101-176 lb.)	90-95 cm. (35-7 in.)
female	35-52 kg. (77-114 lb.)	70-85 cm. (28-33 in.)
Sika (Dorset)		
male	mean 64 kg. (141 lb.)	81 cm. (32 in.)
female	mean 41 kg. (90 lb.)	73 cm. (29 in.)
Roe (Dorset)		
male	mean 26 kg. (57 lb.)	64-7 cm. (25-6 in.)
female	mean 24 kg. (53 lb.)	63-7 cm. (25-6 in.)
Water Deer (Cambs.)		
male	mean 14 kg. (31 lb.)	60 cm. (24 in.)
female	mean 12 kg. (26 lb.)	50 cm. (20 in.)
Muntjac (S. England)		
male	10-18 kg. (22-40 lb.)	44-52 cm. (17-20 in.)
female	9-15 kg. (19-33 lb.)	43-52 cm. (17-20 in.)

47

Top gear

The deer are one of several families of hoofed mammals, collectively known as ungulates. Those that walk on an even number of toes (two in the case of deer) are termed artiodactyls and most of the families in this group are ruminants (i.e. they have a four-chambered stomach and chew the cud). But many mammals are ruminants and have hooves. What is unique to the deer, their very own logo or family crest, is the presence of antlers. Other ruminants such as antelopes, sheep, goats and cattle have horns, so what is the difference between horns and antlers?

Horns: once a horn has grown it is a permanent structure which increases during the animal's life. Indeed, annual rings on the surface can be used to assess the age of some horned animals. A horn consists of two parts. On the outside is a sleeve of horn (hence the name for the whole structure) which is easily separated after the death of the animal. Chemically this is keratin, the same substance of which hooves, fingernails and hair are made: the horn is produced by modified hair follicles.

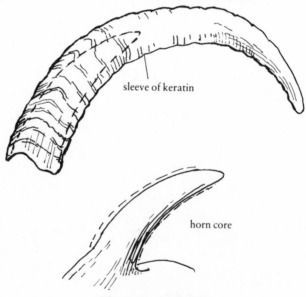

sleeve of keratin

horn core

The structure of a horn.

On the living animal there is, hidden within the covering of keratin, a bone that forms the core of the structure. This core grows out from the frontal bone which forms the forehead part of the skull and remains alive throughout the animal's life. In most species females as well as males have horns which may be straight, curved, coiled or spiral, but not branched.

Antlers: although a deer's head-gear may look like horns the similarity is only superficial. Firstly, antlers do not grow directly from the skull. Before the first pair can grow they need a base from which to sprout. This stalk or 'pedicle', as it is called, is a short outgrowth from the frontal bone and is covered by skin and hairs like those on the rest of the head. The pedicle begins to grow some time within the deer's first year and remains as a permanent structure throughout the animal's life but becomes progressively shorter when the deer gets older.

Once the pedicle has grown, antler development can begin on the top of the pedicle. The antler is made from bone and while it is growing it must have a source of oxygen and food. These are supplied via blood vessels within the growing bone and within the skin that covers the surface of the growing antler. This special skin, which also contains nerves, is called velvet because of its texture: the hairs clothing it are short and erect and unlike hairs anywhere else on the animal.

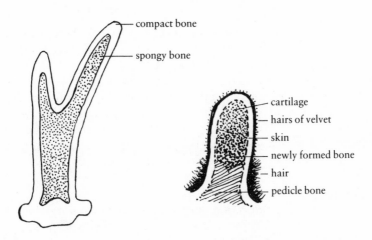

Longitudinal sections of typical antlers: (left) *a dead cast antler and* (right) *an early stage of growth.*

When the antler is fully grown the velvet becomes redundant. It dries and dies and the deer rubs it off against trees or other vegetation. During this stage tatters of messy blood-stained skin may briefly dangle over the deer's face. The blood supply inside the antler is also cut off and the antler becomes dead bone, incapable of further increase in size and unable to replace any portion that may break off later.

In less than a year this pair of antlers falls off and the process begins all over again. The annual growth of the new bone, skin, blood vessels and even nerves in the velvet skin is remarkable and unparalleled in the animal kingdom. Growth occurs at an amazing rate in some species. In moose, 417 g. (15 oz.) a day has been recorded and wapiti antlers may increase by 275 mm. (over an inch) a day. In the deer with small antlers the increase may be only 1 mm. (1/16 in.).

As horns and antlers are completely different structures, 'horn' should not be used for the head adornment of any deer. Old books, including the classic *British Deer and their Horns*, written in 1897 by J. G. Millais, did muddle the terms, and still one hears the term 'in hard horn' meaning the deer has fully grown antlers free of velvet. The Horn Dance celebrated annually in Abbots Bromley on a Monday in September should really be the Antler Dance. Six men, each carrying a pair of reindeer antlers, dance through the town. Why reindeer in the West Midlands? Still, after three hundred years of the custom the name of the festival is hardly likely to be changed.

Men only: with antlers a 'males only' rule applies — females lack them except in the reindeer (caribou). There is a further exception to the family rule. Chinese water deer have no antlers at all. Nor do the musk deer but they are not regarded as true deer. Various anatomical differences, such as having two (instead of four) nipples and possessing a gall bladder cause them to be placed in a separate, but closely related, family. Unfortunately for them the possession by the males of a specialized gland on the abdomen has meant that they have been exploited in Asia for thousands of years for musk which is used in perfumery and medicines.

Antlers great and small

As a general rule, large deer are social animals which form herds, have large breeding groups and carry big antlers. Deer with little antlers, like pudu and muntjac, are of small body size, are mostly solitary and do not form breeding groups.

The largest antlers that ever existed belonged to the giant deer,

A cow reindeer, which has not yet cast her antlers, suckling her calf.

Megaloceros giganteus, but of the present-day species the longest antlers are those of the American wapiti and the tundra caribou, some of which exceed 1.5 m. (5 ft) in length. The Alaskan moose is a much larger animal, taller and heavier than both of these and the extinct giant deer, but its antlers are shorter. They may reach a length of 1.2 m. (4 ft.) and have a broad flattened palm, about 60 cm. (2 ft.) wide. At the other end of the antler scale are those of the tufted deer of Asia, so small that they are hidden in a bunch of hairs which grow from the pedicles. The spikes of the pudu are also very small, about 8 cm. (3 in.)

The deer in Britain have antlers intermediate between these extremes. The smallest are those of the **muntjac** for which a large antler weighs around 20 g. (less than an oz.) and may be 10 cm. (4 in.) long. The **red** stag has the largest with maximum sizes in the wild in Britain being over a metre (*c.* 3½ ft.) long and weighing about 4 kg. (9 lb.) each. Scottish red deer generally have much poorer antlers than those elsewhere in Europe where red stags regularly grow much larger and heavier antlers.

Although the basic pattern of the antlers is fixed for each species, characters inherited from both parents and the quality of food available influence their exact form and size. Some very interesting studies were made during the 1930s in Europe which showed the over-riding importance of food. Red and roe were fed on natural fodder plus a specially formulated diet, high in all the substances required for bone (including antler) formation. When the stags of the third generation were only six years old, two years short of their peak, their body and antler weights were nearly twice what these had been for the original stock. Their antlers ranked among the best in Europe and the results from the roe were similar.

There are several scoring systems used by stalkers to assess and compare antlers. The system used in Europe is the CIC (Conseil International de la Chasse) International Formula. Bronze, silver or gold medals are awarded to the heads achieving the requisite scores. These ratings are purely man-

The long antlers of a North American wapiti and the tiny spikes of a pudu.

'All my own work.'

made assessments which even include marks for beauty: they do not reflect the biological value of the antlers to the wearer. In the view of cynical biologists the glory sometimes appears to reflect upon the stalker rather than on the animal that grew them. National and international exhibitions of trophy antlers are staged periodically when over a thousand red deer heads, also roe and fewer fallow may be submitted. The highest scoring antlers of red and fallow are mostly from eastern Europe, especially Hungary, Yugoslavia, Romania and Bulgaria.

Antler cycles

The growth and casting of antlers is a cyclical event. Within each species the same stage occurs at the same time each year, but with some slight variation between individuals and also between years for the same animal. Both antlers may fall off on the same day or some days apart. Here are the casting dates in successive years for one muntjac buck:

Left antler	Right antler
June 10th	June 18th
June 24th	June 27th
June 13th	June 18th
May 21st	May 13th
May 25th	May 26th

Let us consider the antler cycle of **red, sika** and **fallow** in Britain or indeed anywhere in the northern hemisphere. Any readers from Down Under will realize that their deer will be six months out of phase with ours, but in the northern hemisphere the young are born in May-June and the males grow their pedicles during their first winter or spring. The first antlers grow during the following months and the velvet is shed in late summer, at more or less the same time as that of the older males. The hard antlers are retained by all the males until the following April-June when they are cast. The cycle begins again and will continue year by year throughout the life of the male deer. Observations in Richmond Park on known-age (ear-tagged) fallow bucks showed that the following were the mean dates for casting in this population.

2nd head	June 6th
3rd head	May 21st
4th head	May 10th
later heads	May 1st

but the mean dates for shedding the velvet, including first heads, were all from August 26th to 31st.

The antler cycle of adult **muntjac** follows the same basic pattern. Casting occurs in May, June or early July and velvet is shed in August-September, but they differ from the other species regarding the development of the pedicles and the first pair of antlers. These may begin

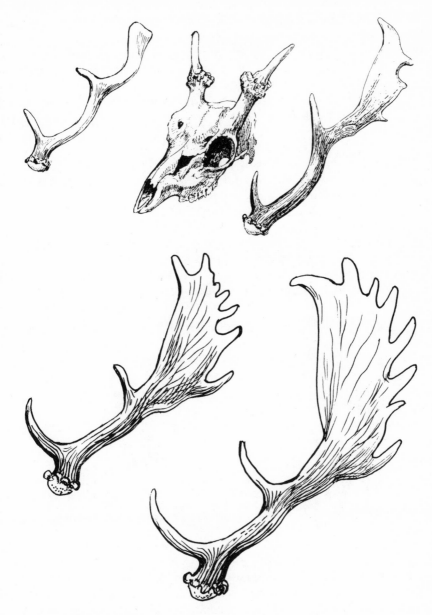

Fallow deer skull (length 23 cm./9 in.) with first, spike antlers and examples of a second, a third and later antlers showing increasing palmation.

to grow, and the velvet may be shed, in any month of the year. This difference occurs because, unlike the others which have a fixed breeding season, muntjac may be born in any month. The age at first casting may be as young as 51 weeks or as old as 112 weeks, but it always occurs in May-June.

For the **roe buck** the seasons for the events are different. The antlers are cast in November-December so the new ones are in velvet during the winter months. That is probably why the velvet is so very much more dense and has longer hairs: to provide a better insulated covering for the growing antlers during the frosty months. The velvet is cleaned in April so the bucks are in hard antler well before the rutting season which, for this species, is in the summer.

Although both sexes of **reindeer** carry antlers they do not both follow the same antler cycle. The bulls cast their antlers after the rut in early winter, perhaps because their extra weight would be an impediment in heavy snow. The females retain their lighter, smaller antlers until late spring but of the cows it is the barren ones which cast earlier than those that are pregnant. This suggests that the antlers are a positive advantage to the females in winter, especially those in greatest need, in helping them compete with the males for the limited food supply and in defence against predators.

"Mind my velvet!"

Reindeer bulls cast their antlers in early winter.

What causes antlers to fall and new ones to grow?
There is a very close association between the stage of the antler cycle and the reproductive organs which also undergo an annual cycle of events. Testosterone, the principal male hormone which is secreted by the testes, plays the prime role. Casting occurs when the testosterone level is lowest

and new antler growth begins while it is still low. Indeed, if a male deer is castrated while in hard antler he will soon cast and then grow a new pair. The castrate, however, will not clean the velvet from his new antlers because this normally occurs when the testosterone secretion increases, nor will he cast this new pair. In the normal entire male, after the antlers are cleaned testosterone secretion and sperm production continue to rise, reaching a maximum at the peak of the mating season. Testicular activity then gradually declines and casting occurs some months later.

This is the basic pattern of events in the deer of temperate regions which have well defined seasons. Even when late conceptions occur outside the main mating season (as evidenced, for example, by occasional births of fallow in autumn instead of June) they have happened during the hard antler phase of the cycle.

Many physiological processes are involved in the antler cycle, some triggered by external factors, especially day-length. Although much has been learned, the whole phenomenon of antler growth remains a fertile field for further research. Muntjac are of special interest because although the antlers show a definite seasonal cycle, breeding occurs all year. Different fascinating problems are posed by the reindeer, partly because the females also have antlers and the oxen (castrated males) do cast and re-grow antlers annually.

A fallow buck looking very messy for some hours while he sheds the velvet from his antlers.

Why have antlers?

The whole business of growing antlers which will be cast a few months later and then repeating the process all over again might at first seem wasteful as well as extraordinary. One reason is that if an antler is to be of use to its owner its size needs to keep in step with the growth of the animal's body. But, instead of being cast, couldn't the antlers grow bigger each year, as horns do? This is not an alternative available to the deer. The antler has been dead for months and further growth would be impossible. The only way to obtain a bigger pair of antlers is to throw off the old and grow a new set.

The possession of antlers is obviously sufficiently important to be worth all the complex biochemical, histological, physiological and behavioural changes associated with casting and new growth. Not surprisingly, most of the behavioural studies concerned with antlers have been of those deer, like red and reindeer, which form large social groups and have evolved the most complex antlers. For these species a number of inter-related roles are fulfilled by antlers. In the less social, small-antlered deer with different mating behaviours these roles are less developed.

Antlers serve as an advertisement hoarding, drawing the attention of other deer to the stag. The more impressive the antlers (which generally go with a bigger body size), the more respected their owner will be and the higher his position in the social hierarchy.

At antler casting time the established dominance order breaks down and for several weeks there are frequent changes in the pecking order. This is because older stags cast first, so temporarily, while the big boys are antlerless, the uncast youngsters rise in the ranks. Any aggressive encounters while the antlers are in velvet will be settled by boxing with the front feet, as hinds do.

The hierarchy isn't fully re-established until all the males have grown and cleaned their new antlers. To sort out this order many sparring contests take place. These are gentle encounters which stop short of proper fights so, without risk of injury, they enable pairs of stags to push and shove with their antlers, assessing their strength and capabilities with others of various sizes.

The sorting out of who is above and who is below in rank takes place before the rut, so in the rutting season, fights usually only occur between evenly matched stags. Indeed, there are further activities they can engage in before having a full-blown fight (see page 79).

During these preliminaries **red, fallow, reindeer**, Père David and other herd species intimidate other males, their potential rivals for the favours of the females, by showing off their antlers, displaying them at various angles by appropriate movements of the head. They know it is much safer to use their antlers offensively in ritualized behaviour rather than defensively in a real fight. The latter can result in serious damage as well as the loss of the ladies.

Fallow bucks have been observed to knock apples off trees with their antlers and one enterprising fallow, a young captive male, learned to chop himself a snack of carrots by using his long spikes to swing the handle of a root-chopper that stood, partly loaded, in his paddock. Unfortunately for him, after a few successes he broke an antler, for dead antler is rather brittle which is why one often sees broken tines. Antlers are also useful as back-scratchers, extending to those parts the hooves can't reach, and make good plastering tools for the stags that wallow in mud (see p.82).

Antler abnormalities

Not surprisingly, for a structure whose formation depends upon many processes, occasionally something goes wrong. Many, but not all, the resulting abnormalities are hormonal in origin.

Sometimes a roe buck looks as though he's wearing a shaggy hat or wig. The unfortunate buck has suffered an injury which has in effect castrated him and, without testosterone, the antlers go on growing so the velvet is never shed. The antler bone, and the velvet covering it, proliferate and cascade over the buck's eyes, making his head grotesque and sometimes blinding him. Within a year or two he dies, usually from infection in the massive growth. This condition, *known as 'perruque' (or 'peruke'), occurs far more frequently in wild roe than in any other species of deer. On the rare occasions that perruque fallow or red deer have been seen the extra growth was more restricted and did not tumble down over the face.*

A perruque roe buck, Hampshire, 1973.

A roe doe can also have a hormonal imbalance which causes her to develop small antlers. This is more likely to occur in middle age but, provided her female hormones are still being produced normally, she is capable of breeding. One case of an antlered female has been reported for moose in Sweden but the condition appears to be very rare except in roe.

A roe doe with pedicles.

The occurrence in fallow of 'double-heads' is well known in Germany and Denmark but has yet to be reported in Britain. The first antlers fail to cast before the second pair begin to grow. Rare cases have occurred in German roe.

Successive sets of antlers are generally larger and heavier than those of the previous year. The final pair, however, may look abnormal and are said to have 'gone back'. For instance, a park red deer, ear-tagged as a calf and therefore of known age, produced good antlers until he was nine years old. The tenth pair was entirely different: one antler was 13 cm. (5 in.), the other 36 cm. (14 in.) long and there were no tines at all. Although this stag was shot he would probably have died before much longer.

Various other abnormalities can occur as a result of injury during the growth of the antlers. The cause of the aptly named corkscrew antlers, occasionally reported in roe and fallow, is uncertain although an association with heavy burdens of internal parasites has been suggested.

Lack of antlers is an abnormality which not infrequently occurs in red deer. Some males fail to develop antlers yet they have all the other

A red deer hummel with the physique of a stag but no antlers.

male characteristics. These 'hummels', as they are called, are capable of breeding and their sons grow normal antlers. Many hummels begin to develop pedicles but their growth is arrested so antlers fail to grow. In later life the antler growth can be stimulated by damage to the top of the pedicle.

Although reports of hummels seem to come mostly from areas of low quality feed, poor nutrition at the time of puberty only partly explains it because their body sizes and weights are comparable to those of antlered males. Hummelism has also been reported in roe bucks, but much less frequently.

Antlers in the service of man

Before the discovery of metals, antlers must have been one of man's most treasured possessions. Without any fashioning an antler could serve as a pick or a hoe. Other uses, such as combs and bridle pieces, required some skill in their preparation and followed later. In modern times antlers have been used for a great variety of decorative purposes from chandeliers to chairs.

Although pieces of antler are commonly found during archaeological excavations, very little study has been made of these finds. The exception is the supply of several hundreds of almost whole red deer antlers found at Grimes Graves in Norfolk, one of the best known Neolithic (New Stone Age) sites in Britain. Despite the name, these are not burial sites but flint mines worked some 5,000 years ago. Over a period of around 400 years several hundred vertical shafts were made through the chalk. When the miners reached the

level at which there were blocks of black flint of the finest quality for tool-making they dug horizontal galleries radiating from the shaft. Working in the cramped, low galleries, the Neolithic men used the antlers, mostly naturally cast ones, as picks to extract the lumps of flint from the chalk rock in which they were embedded.

The tips of the antlers would soon have become blunt from wear and therefore less efficient at prising out the flint, so frequent replacement of the antlers would have been necessary. Various estimates, ranging from one hundred to four hundred, have been made for the number of antlers required to work one mine for one year. It has even been suggested that the deer were herded or enclosed to ensure an easy supply of antlers. Confining large herds and obtaining sufficient food for them would have been an enormous task, and seemingly unnecessary because at that time

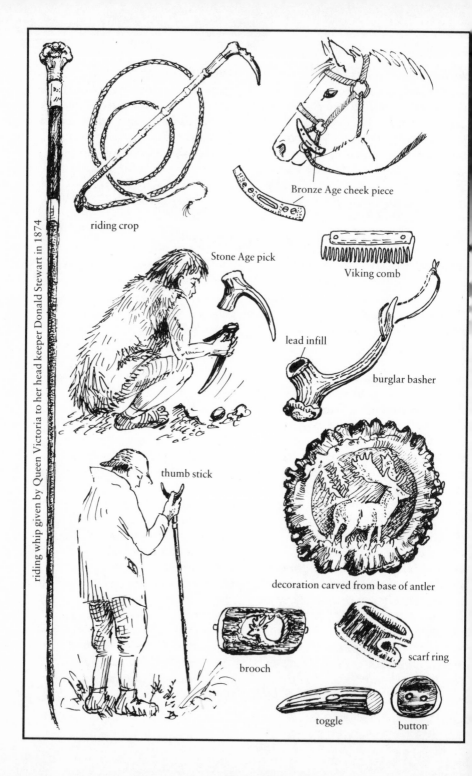

riding whip given by Queen Victoria to her head keeper Donald Stewart in 1874

riding crop

Bronze Age cheek piece

Stone Age pick

Viking comb

lead infill

burglar basher

thumb stick

decoration carved from base of antler

brooch

scarf ring

toggle

button

the local forests would have supported thousands of red deer. The local folk would have known where the stag groups were at casting time and could have collected the antlers with relative ease.

More recently, antlers have been put to very different use: monitoring contamination. Environmental scientists can determine the amounts of various chemicals in antlers; the great benefit is that most of the contamination will have occurred during the growth period of the antler — 130 days or so for a roe buck. (But not all: it is possible for minerals from the skeleton to be mobilized and incorporated into the growing antlers, so any contamination in the skeleton may be passed into the antlers.) About a fifth of the dry weight of an antler is calcium and about a tenth is phosphorus, but traces of other elements can be measured also. The same tests on any other bone would first require the animal to be dead!

Radioactive fallout from atomic weapons tests in the late 1950s was the first type of contamination to be monitored in antlers. Subsequently the main elements measured in antlers were those emitted from industrial processes. In 1979 Polish scientists showed that the amounts of lead, zinc, cadmium, chromium and iron were significantly higher in roe deer from polluted forests than in the Białowieza Forest on the north-east border of Poland. The polluted areas lay in the direction of the prevailing winds coming from the industrial region of Silesia. Vast numbers of deer are shot each year (e.g. over 30,000 roe a year in Poland alone) and many of the males finish up as trophies on a wall, so it is possible to compare present-day data with samples from animals killed decades earlier. Scientists in many other countries began to use tiny samples from antlers as one means of monitoring contaminants in the environment.

Roe antlers were used in Sweden to monitor the levels of heavy metals in two forests. One was situated down-wind from the urban area of Stockholm, the other was near to an area where copper, silver and lead are mined. Antlers from the latter location had constant levels of cadmium and zinc over a fifteen-year period, ending in 1983, but the lead levels declined. A greater fall in lead content was found in antlers from the forest north-east of Stockholm. There the lead level was a third of what it had been ten years earlier. This welcome reduction correlated well with the reduction in lead emissions from the exhaust of motor vehicles. Next time you fill up with lead-free petrol remember the role of antlers in assessing such changes!

Wind can disperse contaminants

over vast distances, depositing them several countries or even continents away from their place of origin. Acid rain and also caesium 137 from the Chernobyl disaster are recent well known examples of this occurrence. Reindeer, moose, roe and red deer have been used as monitors of the levels of radioactivity in several countries affected by the fallout, but in these cases muscle (meat), liver and kidneys were used to measure the number of units of radioactivity per kilo. One might think that the Isle of Rhum, 12 miles (19 km.) off the west coast of Scotland, was well clear of pollutants, but here too pollutants can be blown in; monitoring of lead levels from the antlers of red deer showed a decline betwen 1970 and 1985 although there was no drop in cadmium content.

Antlers can be used to measure other pollutants: some were used in a regional comparison of the amount of fluoride present in animal tissues. Most previous studies had used the bones of farm stock because incidents of fluoride poisoning had occurred in cattle and sheep. This time deer jaw bones and antlers were analysed. The jaws had higher levels than the antlers, as one would expect because they had grown over a longer period. Of the five populations of deer sampled, the highest levels of fluoride were in Thetford Forest, 43 miles (70 km.) north-east of extensive, long-established brickworks, a known source of fluoride emissions, with no other sources between them. This work seems to explode an earlier claim that airborne fluoride is not carried more than 6 miles (10 km.) from its place of origin. Much must depend upon the direction of the prevailing wind and the topography. When monitoring radioactivity in Norway after the Chernobyl accident, large variations were found in different populations of deer which were separated by relatively short distances but which occupied differently facing slopes of the mountains.

'That's a weight off my mind!'

Social or solitary

Some deer move around together in groups and feed close to each other. These are generally the larger species which mainly feed in open habitats where there are plenty of the right food plants close together. Of the deer in Britain the **fallow, red** and **sika** fall within this category, as do the **reindeer.** The number occurring together varies from a handful to scores or hundreds but does not exclude the likelihood of an individual being alone occasionally: for example a female before she gives birth. For much of the year the males and females live in separate groups, each with its own hierarchy, sometimes miles apart. As the mating season approaches the males move to the areas occupied by the females.

In contrast to these gregarious species the **roe, water deer** and **muntjac** exemplify the solitary life-style. These solitary species are smaller and browse or nibble plants more selectively. There would be a disadvantage in a group of them all trying to feed together, competing for a more limited and scattered supply of tasty morsels.

During a study in Dorset, of almost 2,500 sightings of roe bucks believed to be over two years old, 76 per cent were alone. The same percentage of sightings of adult does were either alone or with kids. The other sightings were of twos or threes, mixed or separate sexes and various ages.

At Woodwalton Fen 61 per cent of over 2,000 sightings of water deer were of individuals alone. This may surprise anyone who has watched these deer on the farm field within Whipsnade Wild Animal Park. Here dozens may be feeding together. The explanation is that single deer or mothers with fawns have gone into the field independently, not as a cohesive herd, because it offers the best food. Similarly several muntjac may visit a favoured feeding place, like a carrot field where small succulent roots remain on the surface after harvesting. Each deer has arrived alone and will go his/her own way after a feed.

During a long-term study in the King's Forest, of more than 2,000 sightings of adult female muntjac and over 1,000 of adult bucks about 80 per cent were solitary. The next highest (about 10) percentage was for an adult of each sex together, defined as within 10 m. (33 ft.) of each other. Sightings of three muntjac together were not common and four together were rare. Although generally going about their business alone, a number of muntjac will live in close proximity. For adult muntjac the home range,

Hinds in the Highlands, their legs blended into the bleached grass in March.

the area within which the animal normally confines its day-to-day activities, remains virtually the same all through the year. The home ranges of several females may overlap and a buck's range will include that of several does. When two muntjac are together mutual grooming of the head is a frequent activity. Particular attention is given to the pedicles of males and the ears, including any ear tags (inserted to identify individuals in a study area) which sometimes become very chewed.

Grazers and browsers

Some deer, such as **fallow**, feed mainly on grass but, although they are primarily grazers, they will take some browse. Similarly those that are mainly browsers, like **muntjac** and **roe**, feeding on the leaves of trees and shrubs, will take some grass. This mostly occurs in the spring when the new flush of grass is succulent and the deciduous bushes and trees as yet have little to offer. Fruits such as acorns, beech mast, chestnuts, blackberries, haws and hips are eaten by most of our deer when they are available. In a good nut year more than half a fallow's diet in November in the New Forest consisted of acorns and other fruits. In a poor year, in the same month, fruits accounted for only five per cent of the diet, the rest being made up of grasses, heather, holly, bramble and conifers.

The wide range of food taken by **red** deer shows how this species can adapt to what is available within different habitats. As red deer were, and still are in many countries, animals of forest or forest edge it is not surprising that the buds and leaves of various deciduous trees are especially liked. Analysis of faecal pellets from a part of Thetford Forest, on the Norfolk/Suffolk border, which included conifer and broad-leaved plantations, shrubs and a varied ground flora, showed that in summer the red deer took mostly deciduous leaves (oak, hawthorn, ash, birch and beech), grasses and some bramble. In winter they increased the intake of grasses, and ivy and bramble became major components of the diet. Year-round a total of only twenty-one species of plants, plus an 'others' category, were identified in the pellets. Yet many red deer in Britain live in treeless habitats. Over much of Scotland they take large amounts of heather and other moorland plants to supplement the grasses and rushes they can find. Large brown seaweeds form part of the diet of red deer which have access to the shore. So the diet of a Highland red deer is very different from one living in woodland in southern England.

Bramble is an important food for several species of deer. For much of the year it remains green and the new growth begins early in the spring. In the same area of Thetford Forest used for the red deer pellet analysis the diet of **roe** consisted of the same number of plant species but there was very little seasonal variation. All through the year bramble was the major component of every sample, with sheep's fescue grass, stinging nettles and other grasses as the only other major species. A few miles away in the King's Forest, in very similar habitat, every roe stomach examined was full

A group of stags, well separated from the hinds, in the Highlands.

of bramble and little else.

A study of the pellets of **muntjac** in the King's Forest showed that all year bramble accounted for about forty per cent of the diet. Other foods, however, showed considerable seasonal variation according to whether deciduous leaves, herbs, nuts or fungi were available. Grasses were only important when the preferred plants were not available. Eighty-six species of plants were recognized in the pellets, four times as many as for roe and red in similar habitats. Even allowing for this investigator perhaps having identified more fragments, the other workers who analysed the red and roe deer pellets were hardly likely to have lumped as many as sixty-five species into their 'others' category.

Fungi are part of the autumn diet for many deer. Certainly a variety of species are found in the stomachs of **fallow** and **muntjac**. Toadstools such as *Rozites caperata* (which is edible for humans) and species of *Lactarius* were probably the major source of radioactivity in moose and reindeer in Norway in 1988. Grazing animals had been monitored since the Chernobyl disaster in 1986 and had more or less stable levels of caesium 137 in that year, 1987 and 1989, but there was a dramatic rise in 1988. This coincided with a season of abundance for these fungi which were found to contain up to a hundred times as much of the isotope as green vegetation.

Reindeer have a very specialized diet and must be the only mammals for which lichens are the main food for much of the year. Some shaggy lichens grow on trees, but those on soil or rocks are mostly flat and leaf-like or crisp and wiry. Often these are the only plants over vast areas of bleak habitats where they form grey, brown or pale green carpets. One of the most important is *Cladonia rangiferina* which is commonly, but misleadingly, called reindeer moss. It is not related to the mosses but, like all lichens, consists of a fungus and an alga united in a very specialized form of plant life.

Although all deer are herbivores, there are many reported cases of deer chewing antlers or, more rarely, other bones. The habit is not universal but has been reported in red deer, Roosevelt's wapiti, mule deer, muntjac, axis deer and probably most often in reindeer. Recycling the minerals direct to the deer certainly makes sense.

Another more restricted occurrence of bone-eating in deer has been reported from Rhum where red deer were seen to kill manx shearwater chicks by biting and shaking them. The head, wing bones and leg bones were then eaten. The estimate for the percentage of chicks killed in this way was 0.7. On two occasions I have seen a captive muntjac buck chew the leg bones of a small bird, killed but left intact by a cat. As reported for the red deer, the leg bones were so neatly removed that the claws were still connected to the body by a strand of skin and tendons. Presumably these habits are a response to the need for additional calcium, phosphorus or other substances within the bones.

Chewing the cud

'Chewing it over' is a familiar expression when we want to take a little time to mull over a problem. For deer, and other cud-chewers such as cattle, sheep, goats and antelopes, the process is an essential part of everyday life. The alternative name for the process is 'rumination'.

A ruminant's stomach has four distinct compartments. The first and largest, except in young deer being suckled, is the rumen. The second, much smaller, is the reticulum, the lining of which has a beautiful, raised net-like pattern similar to that on the coat of a reticulated giraffe. The third chamber is the omasum. Although small, this has its internal surface area increased enormously by flat, broad folds which resemble the pages of a book. Its old fashioned name was psalterium (psalm book) and some stalkers still refer to it as 'the Bible'. Lastly is the abomasum which has an almost smooth lining and is equivalent to the stomach of other mammals.

The vegetation is plucked using the lower spatula-like front teeth against the hard pad at the front of the roof of the mouth, there being no upper front teeth. After only partial chewing, the food is swallowed and passes into the rumen which acts as a temporary storage bag in which the

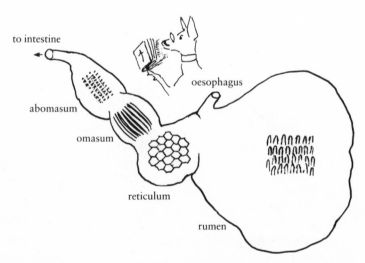

The four-chambered stomach of a deer, showing the lining typical of each compartment.

food is churned about and mixed with saliva. Having eaten its fill the deer can then retreat to a safe place to ruminate. For this they usually lie down.

A ball of food, the cud, is regurgitated into the mouth. The side to side action of the jaws ensures that the food is ground between the ridges of the cheek teeth. That mouthful of food, mixed with saliva, passes back down the gullet to continue its passage through the rest of the stomach. Up comes the next ball of food, as can be seen if you have a good view of the neck of a ruminating animal.

The lining of the rumen has thousands of tiny finger-like projections so its surface area is increased tremendously. Within the rumen and reticulum is a vast work force of micro-organisms. These bacteria and protozoa are vital to the working of a ruminant's digestion. It is they that break down the cellulose (a carbohydrate) which forms the walls of plant cells. Great volumes of methane and carbon dioxide are produced in the rumen but there are mechanisms for getting rid of these gases: some are expelled through the mouth as a silent belch and some pass down the windpipe, into the lungs, and are absorbed into the blood. The abdomen of a dead ruminant soon becomes bloated, because fermentation in the rumen does not cease immediately upon death, but the removal of the gases does.

Deer are inquisitive creatures and their exploration of novel things does unfortunately include the ingestion of unsuitable objects. Polythene and plastic string are the most common hazards these days but balloons, elastic bands and even disposable knickers are among the items that have been found. These indigestible objects remain in the rumen or reticulum where they may cause a blockage. Of over eighty wild fallow from Essex whose stomachs were examined about half contained one or more foreign bodies.

Pluckers, grinders and tusks

An animal's survival can depend upon its teeth. If they fail to cope with the diet malnutrition results, debilitation follows and the animal gradually fades away. If a stalker cuts open the heart of a deer that died in poor condition he may find a 'chicken-fat' clot of blood, so called from its yellow colour. This is a sure sign that life has slowly ebbed away: worn-out teeth may be the indirect cause.

In any deer with a full set of permanent teeth there are, in each lower jaw, four at the front, then a large gap followed by three premolars and three molars. The upper teeth consist of the three premolars and three molars; their cusps fit into the troughs of the teeth below and vice versa so vegetation can be ground between them when the jaws move from side to side. All these teeth except the molars are preceded by deciduous (milk) teeth. The front teeth are often referred to as the incisiform teeth because, although the first three are incisors, the fourth is really a canine in disguise.

The white enamel layer of the teeth gradually becomes worn away and cannot be replaced. Consequently the underlying brown dentine becomes increasingly exposed as the crown becomes flatter, smoother and less

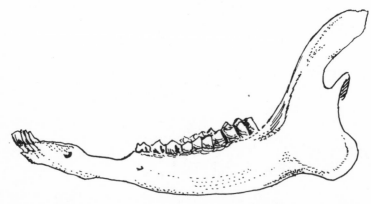

Left jaw bone with permanent dentition: the number and arrangement of these teeth is the same in all species of deer.

efficient at grinding. Eventually in very old deer the crown may be only a fraction of an inch tall or may fall out completely.

In addition to these teeth possessed by all deer, some species also have a pair of upper canine teeth. The males of **muntjac**, and even more so those of **water deer** display formidable tusks worthy of a fearsome flesh-eater. In these herbivores the tusks are used as weapons against a rival and for the antlerless water deer their role is especially important. Very efficient they are at the stab and slash technique: a friend of mine caught a muntjac buck, which had crept into a pheasant pen for an easy meal of corn, and had to have twelve stitches in his thigh as a memento!

In the male muntjac the upper canines are the first deciduous teeth to be replaced by a permanent tooth and this happens at about twenty-one weeks of age. In the female the tiny deciduous upper canine is not replaced by a slightly larger permanent one until she is over a year old (53-57 weeks). This is the only tooth in which there is a sex difference in the sequence of eruption. Growth of the tooth in the male is rapid so it is available as a weapon before the buck has worthwhile antlers.

The tusks of muntjac are curved, have a very sharp point, a cutting rear edge and can reach a length of 45 mm. (1¾ in.). These teeth can be moved slightly but not nearly to the same extent as the much bigger tusks of the water deer. A high proportion of muntjac bucks have one or both upper canines broken. Such was the case with 41 per cent of 76 bucks over two years old whose skulls have been examined. The causes of breakage are unknown. Perhaps they rootle around among stones more than we realize.

A radio-collared mature male, known as Red Buck, was re-caught a week after a new buck, with intact tusks, had arrived in a particular study area. Red Buck, whose tusks were broken, had three deep slash wounds; one had penetrated to his pelvis. He was given veterinary treatment on the spot, including antibiotics and sutures, and released. He survived another six years before a car killed him.

In contrast to these mini-sabres are the short, rounded upper canines, called 'tushes', of **red** and **sika** deer, which happen to make attractive tie-pins and ear-rings! **Fallow** and **roe** don't normally have upper canines but occasionally one or a pair are present. In one park a quarter of the fallow fawns had them but they are seldom replaced in the permanent dentition. Another departure from the usual occurs in some fallow which have one or a pair of the lower front teeth absent.

Wildlife biologists and archaeologists may, for various reasons, wish to know the age at death of a deer, perhaps an animal that has been shot, or a long-buried jaw bone. Teeth provide a useful means of assessing age. The sequence of replacement of milk teeth by permanent teeth varies between the species and so does the age at which the permanent set is fully functional. For example:

Red deer	26-33 months
Fallow	27-31 months
Roe	14 months
Muntjac	19-23 months

With knowledge of the age of eruption of each tooth one can estimate the approximate ages of young animals. The task is more difficult for those deer with a full permanent dentition. The rate of wear of the teeth varies among different populations of the same species according to their diet, so ideally one needs jaws from known-aged animals from the same locality for comparison. The effect of different diets can be very marked indeed. Captive deer fed on unnatural foods, such as hard grains and pulses instead of grass or browse, can wear out their teeth many years earlier than a wild deer.

Using jaws from red and fallow of exactly known ages from one park, a method has been devised for scoring the wear of teeth. A point was given for wear on and between each slope of each molar tooth. The total score was the same or very similar for deer of the same age and same species. In some areas, where there is a marked difference between the seasons, it is possible to distinguish growth lines in the cementum which surrounds the root of a tooth, rather like the annual rings of a tree. The tooth (first molar, or sometimes an incisor is used) must be extracted, cut and polished. The technique has been used frequently in Scotland and elsewhere but interpreting the lines is not always as easy as it may sound.

Scents, sounds and signals

If your first close encounter with a deer is a rutting red stag or a fallow buck you will think deer are incredibly smelly animals. This is the only time when our noses detect a strong odour, but for the deer themselves smell must be at all times an important means of communication. Whether they are gregarious or solitary they need to know where others are, either to avoid them or to make contact. The latter is especially important between mother and young or for attraction and stimulation between the sexes at the appropriate time.

Within the deer family there are at least thirteen sites on the body at which scent organs may be situated. No one species has glands at all these locations but most deer have several scent organs, which may be active all year or only at certain seasons. The secretions come from specialized sweat and sebaceous glands within the skin. The latter secrete fatty substances and usually open into a hair follicle. There is much yet to be discovered about the chemistry of the secretions and their meanings to deer. In this chapter only the deer present in Britain are discussed.

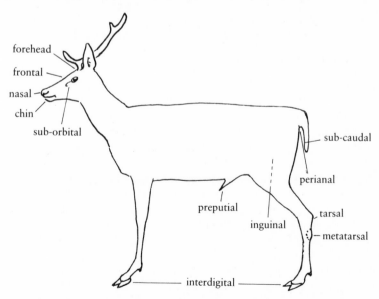

A generalized deer showing the locations of scent glands present in various species.

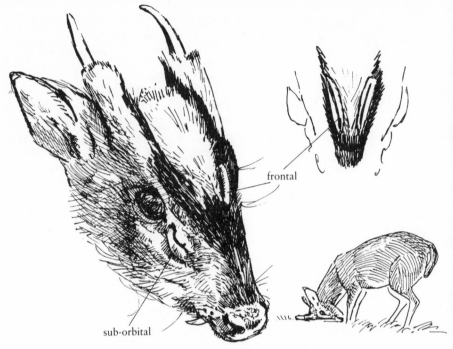

(Left and above right) *Scent glands on the head of a muntjac deer;* (below right) *muntjac buck scent-marking the ground with his frontal glands.*

Heady smells

All our deer have scent-secreting areas just below the corner of the eye. In all except the roe they are seen as a slit or pocket in the skin. In **muntjac** these pockets are very large and conspicuous: the pit in the skull that houses the folds of skin is as big as the eye socket. Very often when a muntjac, buck or doe, urinates or defecates the pockets open, as they do also during courtship of this and other species. Secretions from the eye region are much more limited in the **roe** and nothing obvious marks their location. They are probably restricted to bucks, who use them to deposit scent on posts or previously frayed saplings by rubbing the corner of an eye over the surface. The small size of the sub-orbital pits is a useful feature in distinguishing skulls of roe and water deer of any age from muntjac.

Roe bucks also produce scent from the forehead, but only during the period from when they are setting up territories until the rut. There is no external sign of the glands, which are situated high on the forehead, close to the pedicles. Only **muntjac** have a pair of shallow, secretory grooves on the forehead. These frontal glands are about 3cm. (1in.) long and lie within the black stripes on the head of a buck and the dark marking on a doe. Frequently a deer opens these grooves and wipes the forehead on the ground, evidently leaving a message for another muntjac.

Inside the nose seems a strange place to develop a scent-producing organ but several species of deer have nasal glands, although in Britain the **reindeer** is the only example. The glands consist of folds in the lining of the floor of the nasal passage. Their function is not yet known but presumably the 'lips' that close the opening (which is nearly 3 cm./1 in. long) prevent the animal inhaling its own scent.

Reindeer also have a pair of tarsal glands on the hock. **Red, sika, fallow** and **roe** also have scent-producing areas on the hind legs but theirs are situated below the hock. The position of these metatarsal glands shows clearly as a raised pad of hairs on the outer side of the leg. Those on sika deer in winter coat are especially conspicuous, showing as a white pad against an almost black leg.

Hidden from our view between the two toes that make up the hoof of each hind foot there are scent glands in **reindeer, fallow, roe, muntjac** and **water deer.** In the water deer their location is easily seen as soon as the two cleaves of the foot are parted to reveal a tube-like pocket almost 4 cm. (1½ in.) long. In the other species the glandular sac is shorter and not seen so clearly unless a cut is made between the two toes.

The **fallow** buck's pungent, rutty, never-to-be-forgotten smell comes from his prepuce which changes appearance for the rut and then looks rather like cracked dry earth or the surface of a ginger-nut biscuit. The hairs at the end of his penis sheath become splayed and, like the groins, stained brown with urine. On white bucks this staining is especially obvious. The **red** deer has glandular tissue on the underside of the tail which also produces a strong-smelling tar-like secretion. This tissue is more active in hinds than stags but as yet no correlation with seasonal activities has been discovered.

The **Chinese water deer** has some glands the others don't have. Both sexes have inguinal glands, which can only be seen when the groins are examined. Either side of the mammary tissue there is a comma-shaped patch of almost hairless skin (*c.*45 × 35mm./1½ × 2 in.). Glandular activity occurs all year round and is indicated by the dark, waxy specks of secretion which might at first be regarded as surface dirt, although other deer are remarkably clean in this area.

Raspberries and roars

Most deer have a soft bleat or 'pheep' contact call between young and mother and a louder 'shout for help' if they are seriously disturbed or attacked. It was interesting in a typical park situation to see that when a **red** calf uttered an alarm call many hinds came running to it, not just its own mother. Yet a **fallow** fawn's alarm call was only responded to by its own mother. Are fallow better at recognizing their own infants' voices or are red deer aunts and grandmothers more caring? The social set-up is such that groups of hinds associating together are likely to be mothers, daughters and sisters.

Several species of deer bark. **Fallow** does bark when a fawn is nearby and danger is threatening and occasionally at other times when an adult is disturbed, but they are relatively silent in comparison with roe and muntjac. Both sexes of **roe** bark at any season, often a series of gruff calls uttered after, or while running from, a disturbance, but it is **muntjac** that are sometimes called barking deer. The bucks and does bark at any time if something unfamilar makes them suspicious and especially in the days following the birth of a fawn. Their most commonly used bark is very loud and may be repeated many, even hundreds, of times, with a pause of a second or so between each one.

The grunting, belching groan of a **fallow** buck in autumn as he patrols his rutting area can't be adequately described: even a tape-recording can't convey the atmosphere. One needs to experience it in woodland or field-edge on a misty dawn or a star-lit frosty night. In volume he is surpassed

Roe reactions when suspicious of danger.

A rutting red stag roars across Exmoor.

by the gutteral roar of a rutting **red** stag as he advertises his presence down the glen or through the forest. He is attracting hinds, stimulating them to come into season and warning would-be challengers. Studies on Rhum have shown that stags can assess each other from their roaring performance. If a stag decides from the voice that his opponent is more powerful, then he will not engage in a fight. The act of roaring is itself exhausting and there is no point in wasting energy in a hopeless fight. A stag in his prime may hold a harem for three weeks. During that time some roar, on average, twice a minute throughout the day and night, but before a fight the rate may escalate to eight roars a minute.

By counting the number of stags heard roaring at the height of the rut, a method was devised in Norway for assessing the size of the population. Used in conjunction with observations on the social structure of that population, including average harem size, this proved a useful census technique. The method is especially suitable in forested, mountainous habitats like the south-east corner of Poland where the census figure obtained was more reliable than the traditional and more labour-intensive method of tracking in the snow.

When it comes to the prize for the most unusual range of calls made by a deer, **sika** must be the winners. Their repertoire includes a piercing whistle, made by a stag at rutting time or by hinds with calves, and a very loud 'raspberry'.

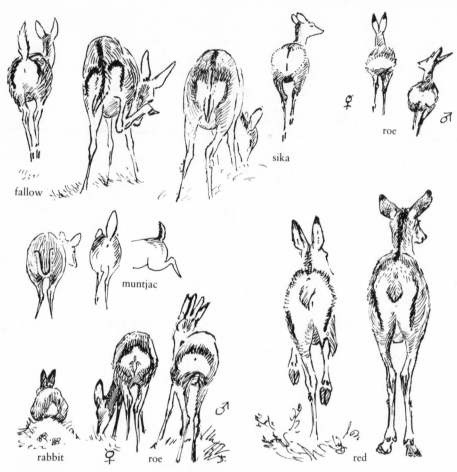

Rear ends of undisturbed and alarmed deer. For most deer species the white signal is a warning to other deer, as it is in rabbits.

Stamps and clicks: not all sounds made by deer originate from the voice-box. Many species, when alarmed, run off thumping the ground. Similarly, foot-stamping, often alternating left and right fore feet, is a common behaviour when deer are unsure of something strange.

A clicking noise is produced by the feet of **reindeer** and Père David deer. To hear one captive reindeer click as it walks is intriguing enough but to hear thousands on migration must be amazing; it has been likened to an enormous orchestra of castanets. Possibly the sound has a value in maintaining contact between members of the herd. A different sort of clicking is made by **muntjac** bucks. It is a clicking or grinding of the teeth sometimes heard when two bucks are being aggressive to each other or when a buck has been startled by someone he hasn't seen.

Tail piece

Other means of communication rely on good visibility. The rumps of some deer are specialized for this purpose. Both **roe** and **sika** have patches of white (cream on roe in summer) which contrast with the rest of the coat. If the deer is alarmed these hairs become erect and the patch looks like an outsize, very conspicuous powder-puff. Other deer seeing their associates fleeing and displaying this warning know that danger threatens.

The **muntjac** lack such a patch but when alarmed they raise the tail vertically like a flag displaying all 14 cm. (5½ in.) of white underside. **Fallow** also raise their tails when alarmed, but in a less rigid manner.

An alarmed roe doe puffs out the hairs of her rump patch; note her anal tuft of hairs.

In a rut

Autumn orgy: autumn is the rutting time for **fallow, red** and **sika** deer. For months the hormones of a male deer have been preparing him for this once-a-year sexual extravaganza which is accompanied by much activity and calling. The rut begins in October but preliminary activities start some weeks earlier when the males move to areas occupied by the females. Here they make scrapes or wallows, thrash bushes and fray or score the bark of trees. They become aggressive to rivals but attentive to the females. Each sexually mature male aims to gather a harem, but in practice often only those of certain status (determined by age, size and physical fitness) succeed in holding a group of females; the males about 16 months old with their first antlers stand little chance. On Rhum the red stags between 5 and 11 years are the most successful. A stag or buck rounds up any female who tries to wander from his group and pursues any male who tries wife-stealing.

Rutting red stags wallowing in mud.

Lonely harts.

In some places **fallow** depart from this general pattern. Instead of a buck gathering his does to his rutting stand, which is well separated from those of other bucks, a number of males assemble close together at a 'lek', a term better known for the mating ground of blackcock. Each buck then has a tiny area to defend and attempts to mate with any does attracted to him or passing through his patch, but each doe probably mates only once. This lekking behaviour has been described in detail for the first time in the last few years and is now known to occur in several places in England (including Petworth Park) and at least one area in Italy: it has been known to happen in the Jaegersborg Dyrehavn near Copenhagen for many years.

Frequently a buck or stag must test whether a female is ready to be mated. This involves sniffing and licking around the rump or tasting her urine. He will then show the very characteristic response for which there is no English word, so we use the German *flehmen*. He raises his head and curls back his lips as he savours the apparently delectable scent.

Males assess each other from their size, antlers and voice. Only when a male thinks himself superior or at least equal does a fight ensue. Having approached, the two males then walk parallel to each other before turning to clash antlers and shove, aiming to dislodge and unbalance their opponent. The challenger may quit while only his pride is injured but if he wins the contest he gains the harem.

All this activity and constant watchfulness spread over two or three weeks leaves very little time for feeding so it is not surprising that red, sika and fallow males lose condition during the rut. A friend of mine who was visiting the New Forest in late October was thrilled to spot a very large, beautifully palmated antler of a fallow buck lying in the bracken. Some five or six months after antler casting time he could hardly believe his luck. As he approached he saw the antler was still attached to a body. When only a few yards away he discovered not a dead buck but one so worn out by the exertions of the rut that he hadn't even attempted to stand.

Winter wooing: the **reindeer** in Scotland rut in November when the bulls move around seeking out receptive cows. When not tending his cows, the bull may thrash vegetation or spar or fight with other males. He advertises his presence with his 'bugle' call and by disseminating his odour by urinating on to his hind feet.

For the duration of the rut the necks of male reindeer, and also **red, sika** and **fallow** deer, become much thicker and the size is accentuated in the first three named by the development of a mane. This increase in size is not associated with deposition of fat, but with the temporary growth of muscle tissue, a very unusual physiological occurrence. Investigation of three neck muscles in reindeer showed that they all became larger, and one increased more then five hundred per cent. The circumference of the neck of a fallow buck killed in Essex during the rut (October) measured 74 cm. (29 in.), which was 10-20 cm. more than on comparable bucks killed at other seasons.

Chinese water deer rut a little later, in December. Noisy chases can be heard as a buck pursues a doe and barking is more frequent than at other times of the year. The bucks use their feet to make scrapes into which they urinate and defecate.

A fight between two equally matched rutting fallow bucks is fast and furious.

The roe rut. The doe has a peculiar gait prior to mating, a slow canter with the hind legs together and the rump raised.

Summer season: **roe** differ from all these autumn or winter breeders by rutting in July-August. Unlike those of red, sika and fallow the antlers of roe are hard at this time of year and in a suitable state for fighting a rival if necessary. In the preceding weeks the bucks have become restless. They have established territories which they patrol, making scrapes, fraying saplings and scent marking. The does become skittish, sometimes dashing about between bouts of feeding. Yearling does come into season first and a buck will spend hours close to such a youngster until she is ready. Furious chasing, often in circles or figures of eight, precede mating and this may be repeated several times. A week or two later mature does become receptive. Each leaves her kids, now without their spots and normally following their mother, to spend an hour or so with a buck. During this time he will mount her several times but there is little chasing.

In mammals, once mating has occurred the fertilized egg implants into the wall of the uterus and begins to grow into the embryo. The very few exceptions to this rule include one deer, the roe. The fertilized egg remains dormant, in a state of suspended animation, for about five months. About the beginning of January it begins to develop in the normal way. This strategy of delayed implantation means that conceptions occur in the summer when the males are in hard antler and sexually most active but, although gestation only lasts five months, the kids are born at the most favourable time of year, May-June. **Red** and **sika** calves are also born May-June; **fallow** fawns in June.

All through the year: **muntjac** are the odd ones out. They have no fixed season for mating and a fawn may be born in any month of the year. Within a day or so of the birth the doe is in season and will usually conceive after vigorous courtship chases by a buck. He repeatedly sniffs and licks her vulval area and, presumably, when he receives the right chemical signal, he mounts her, often many times in succession. Gestation is 210 days, so the doe has the potential to produce a new fawn every seven months, and to keep up this performance over many years. By the time she was fourteen years old one captive doe had produced twenty-two fawns. In the other species the males are sexually active only when their antlers are hard but whether a muntjac has hard or growing antlers he is equally aroused by a receptive doe and is able to fertilize her.

Fallow buck showing flehmen *response after licking a doe's urine.*

Fawns, calves and kids

A newly born deer is fully furred, open-eyed and able to follow its mother almost straight away if necessary. One young at a time is usual for most deer, but there are some notable exceptions to that generalization. Moose, white-tailed deer, mule deer and **roe** frequently produce twins. In Britain about 75 per cent of roe does have twins, 20 per cent have singletons and about 5 per cent have triplets. These figures vary in different areas and also from year to year. A roe doe normally leaves her kids lying up in separate places, no doubt a case of not putting all her eggs in one basket, for a young roe makes a tasty meal for a fox and two would provide a feast. Occasionally red or fallow deer produce twins but the incidence is very low. Twin foetuses have been recorded very rarely in muntjac but I know of no proven cases of live births.

Only one species produces more than three at a time and that is the **Chinese water deer** for which six have been recorded. However, to produce such a large litter is rare and the chances of rearing all would be very slight. In a population living wild in Cambridgeshire up to four foetuses have been found in females killed in accidents. At Whipsnade Wild Animal Park the average number of foetuses was 2.3 but in some years perinatal mortality is as high as fifty per cent.

At birth young deer have a coat heavily dappled with spots, usually of

A young roe kid has a heavily spotted coat.

Chinese water deer fawns; they are born in May or June, after a gestation period of about 176 days.

white or cream hairs but sometimes, as in the case of the black fallow deer, of a paler shade of the background colour. This breaks up the outline of the animal and if it is lying on leaf litter in woodland or among heather and peat hags it is especially well camouflaged. A camouflage jacket is no use unless the wearer's behaviour complements the outfit, so the young deer needs to lie very still and conceal itself under vegetation when it does not match the background. It is amazingly difficult to spot a fawn as large as a fallow (about 4.5 kg./10lb.) or even a red deer calf of twice this weight even if it is only tucked up in bright green longish grass or tussocks of rushes. Newly born muntjac, which have an average birth weight of 1.2 kg. (under 3 lb.) and roe kids, which aren't much bigger, are even more easily hidden. Even those muntjac which are born in the months when there is very little ground vegetation manage to conceal themselves well.

The exceptions to the usual rule of the spotted coat at birth are the rusa deer of Indonesia, moose and **reindeer**. The calves of the last are buff-brown/grey so their colours blend well with rocks, lichens or ground-hugging dwarf trees. Reindeer calves may be born where there is still snow on the ground and while the mothers are still on migration to the tundra, yet within a few hours their calves are able to join the herd on its trek. The milk of deer in general has a high energy density and this is especially so in reindeer; the growth of calves is rapid.

Orphans are rare: nevertheless every year well intentioned people find a young deer and assume that because it is alone it has been abandoned by its mother. Such an assumption is completely illogical. A few moments' thought would surely make them realize that the mother can't, and has no need to, stay with her young all day. The greater part of her day must be spent in alternating bouts of feeding and ruminating to provide for her

Fallow doe suckling and grooming a well-grown fawn; does may suckle for up to nine months.

own nutritional requirements and to meet the very great demands of lactation (which according to species lasts 4 to 9 months). She returns at intervals to suckle the young but will be deterred from doing so if humans, whom she perceives as danger, are nearby. If you do find any young deer just enjoy the glimpse of such a beautiful creature and retreat without touching, which would contaminate it with human scent, or disturbing it.

There are occasional instances of young being orphaned because the mother has been killed in a traffic accident but unless such a circumstance is known for sure any intervention must be resisted. Fawns misguidedly taken into care seldom receive the appropriate diet and many succumb to diarrhoea or deficiencies. For those that do survive there is the follow-on problem of what to do with an animal which has been reared as a pet, is unafraid of humans and perhaps dogs too but is becoming large, heavy and boisterous, needing space and the company of its own kind. Males present a particular problem once they have antlers, sometimes becoming a serious hazard to people and wrecking the fences of their enclosures. For those reared for genuine reasons human contact must be kept to a minimum if there is to be any chance of rehabilitation to a normal life in the wild. Such an aim requires much self-control by the human carer dealing with such an attractive, appealing animal.

Reading the signs

Deer are shy animals, with good reason to avoid encounters with man, his dogs and motor vehicles. Consequently in many of their habitats they are most active at times when they are least likely to meet these potential hazards. So the first indications that deer are about may not be sightings of the animals but signs of their activities, or warnings of their presence.

Man-made signs
The road sign showing a stag indicates that deer of one or another species are in the vicinity. The warning is not heeded by all drivers although the consequences of an impact can be very serious, even fatal for the occupants of the vehicle as well as the animal. In some areas, to try to minimize these accidents, road-side reflector posts have been erected. These reflect headlights into forest on either side of the road to deter deer. On certain stretches of road these are said to have benefited the deer, with a significant reduction in casualties. Nevertheless, thousands are killed on roads every year. The positioning and maintenance of reflector posts is critical. A post overgrown by vegetation or having dirty metal or plastic plates will not project the beam of a vehicle's headlights as it is intended to do.

In some areas where a motorway passes through deer country miles of chain-link fencing have been erected. Users of the M11 and M25 in Essex will be familiar with such fences, as fallow are numerous in the vicinities.

Road reflectors

Road-side reflector posts help to reduce accidents.

The fencing needs to be 2 m. (6½ ft.) high and there must be no gaps at the bottom nor where drainage ditches or bridges meet the fence. Deer sometimes use underpasses provided primarily for farm vehicles. Some other countries, such as the Netherlands, are much further advanced in providing purpose-built cerviducts and wide bridges (40 m./45 yd.) for wildlife to move between portions of forest which have been dissected by new roads.

Deer-made signs

There are plenty of clues to look for in woods, along hedgerows and around edges of fields. Tufts of hair may be left on barbed wire as deer usually prefer to go under or through fences rather than jump them. When trying to identify the hairs remember that summer and winter coat hairs differ in colour, texture and length and that foxes, badgers, hares and dogs may also leave some hairs on the barbs.

Slots: provided the soil is suitably soft or damp, where an animal has passed under a fence wire there are likely to be some footprints. Deer are creatures of habit and very worn paths will be found through undergrowth and where they cross ditches and streams. Practice is required to decide which species of ungulate has left a cloven hoof print. If you think you have found slots (as the footprints of deer are called)

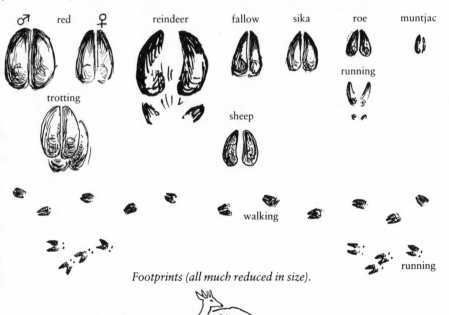

Footprints (all much reduced in size).

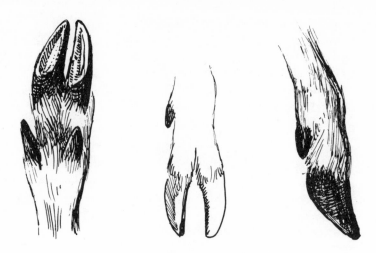

Roe deer foot: actual size from base of dew claws to tip of cleaves is 9.5 cm./3.75 in.

consider first whether there is a flock of sheep around! The daintiest of the deer slots belong to the **muntjac**: they are less than 3 cm. (*c*.1 in.) long. Sometimes, but not always, one cleave is slightly longer than the other and this may show in a really clear-cut slot. The broad slots of a fully grown **red** stag are about 9 cm. (3½ in.) by 7 cm. (2½ in.) wide. The toes, and therefore the slots, of **water deer, roe, sika** and **fallow** fall between these two extremes.

When a deer walks or trots the hind feet step on to the tracks just made by the fore feet, so the slots we see are of overlapping footprints. This registering of one print on another doesn't occur when a deer gallops or jumps. On these occasions the two halves (cleaves) of the hoof are somewhat splayed, with a wider gap between them, and an impression is also made by the dew-claws. These are the mini-hooves situated one each side at the back of the foot, above the level of the cleaves; they are all that remains on the outside to represent two other toes which existed in the ancestors of deer millions of years ago.

Droppings: the droppings of deer can be distinguished easily from those of other wild mammals but deciding which species of deer deposited them needs some practice. Whichever species, the pellets are firm, black or very dark brown. They are short and cylindrical or occasionally more spherical, usually with a little point at one end. The surface is smooth with no fragments of plants visible on the surface, a feature which

red

roe

Typical red deer pellet (on left) *about 2½ cm./1 in. long and 1.5 cm./½ in. wide but some are less pointed or more rounded and several may adhere together; small heap of roe pellets* (on right) *each about 1.5 cm./¾ in. long.*

immediately distinguishes them from the more fibrous and crumbly pellets of hares and rabbits.

Generally the droppings are deposited in a heap of several dozen separate pellets but they may adhere together to form a string or a clump. Amorphous lumps of dung are usually associated with rutting stags and fallow bucks but have been seen at other seasons. As with slots, size is the main difference among the pellets of the different deer species, but there is some overlap in the range of sizes (e.g. **roe / muntjac; fallow / sika**). Those of the **red** stag can be 25 mm. (1 in.) long and over half this width while those of the **muntjac** are 6-13 × 5-11 mm./ (0.2-0.5 × 0.2-0.4 in.).

Wildlife biologists can utilize the droppings of deer in various ways. By counting groups of pellets in sample areas they can compare the use made of different parts of a habitat by one species of deer. If one knows the mean number of times a deer defecates a day and how long the pellets take to decay it is possible, by sampling pellets, to estimate the number of deer in the area. The rate of break-down of droppings will depend partly upon the micro-climate around them.

Determining how often a free-ranging wild deer defecates is not a simple matter and substituting data obtained from observations on a confined deer fed on an unnatural diet would not be appropriate. The mean rate of defecation measured over one week for four muntjac in an extensive paddock and fed on a semi-natural diet of browse, horse chestnuts and carrots was 7.5 times per day. The carrots probably had a higher water content than the plants which the deer would have selected in the wild and this is one factor known to affect frequency of defecation.

Barking up the right tree: the shredded bark of young trees is another sign that deer may be around, but remember that some other mammals damage bark. In autumn, as rutting time approaches, male **red, sika** and

fallow rub and fray slim trunks and thrash branches. A red stag may fray to a height of 120 cm. (40 in.) and the other males to a lower level, proportional to their own height. The tines of the antlers may penetrate into the wood below the bark, leaving score marks. **Roe** buck fraying activity may occur any time between April and August, which includes the times when they are rubbing off velvet, establishing territories and rutting. Fraying by **muntjac** is usually confined to very thin stems which the bucks rub with their teeth at any time of year. The stripping of bark to eat in winter, especially by **red** deer, is a much more serious form of damage to conifer trees than that caused by the males fraying and thrashing.

Don't blame the wrong animal! Deer bites can be distinguished from those of hares and rabbits, by the tell-tale piece of stem that remains.

(Left) *Red hind stripping bark from lodge pole pine; roe buck* (middle) *and red stag* (right) *fraying Scots pine bark.*

Browsed bushes: in deer parks the browse line created by the deer is very distinct and explains why the trees there do not have branches sweeping down to the ground. Similarly in the countryside bushes will be seen sculpted into shape by browsing deer. No one minds if they are hawthorns but the story is different when deer browse the leading shoot and lateral buds from rows and rows of young trees in a commercial plantation.

To enable specially vulnerable species to get established some foresters and gardeners resort to the use of solid-sided plastic tree-guards, the original type being called Tuley tubes after their designer. The warmer, more humid micro-climate within the tubes, which are several feet tall, accelerates growth as well as protecting the shoots from browsing animals. Several variations are now available, but none is as small as the cardboard milk cartons used on Vancouver Island! Apparently these give initial protection to newly planted trees in mountainous terrain occupied by Roosevelt's wapiti and black-tailed deer. In Scotland the presence of a tall fence round a plantation is an indication of the presence of deer, otherwise such a large expense would have been avoided.

Scrapes: another sign that deer are about are the scrapes made by males. At rutting time **red** and **sika** stags make conspicuous depressions in soil.

Natural topiary by red deer in a spruce plantation.

Tree guards give protection.

The diameter of the hollows varies greatly from a foot or so to several metres (yards). A red or sika stag chooses a wet boggy place if possible and creates a wallow into which he sprays his pungent rutty urine before lying down. He may stretch his neck along the ground or roll so that he is thoroughly smeared with mud or soil. When he stands he often uses his dirty antlers to spread the mud, now laden with his scent, over his back. During observations on a sika wallow in Japan one wallow was used eighteen times by six stags during October-November. At other times of the year these mud baths are used by hinds as well as stags, especially when they are shedding their winter coats and probably feel itchy.

Fallow bucks dispense with the mud wallow but they too paw at the ground to make depressions of various sizes in leaf litter, grass or damp patches of soil. They urinate into at least some of the scrapes and may then use their antlers to smear some of the smelly soil on to the body. Use of the scrapes ceases after the rut and gradually they become filled with fallen leaves or overgrown by grass.

The scrapes made by **roe** bucks while establishing their territories in the spring are mostly around 30 cm. (a foot) across. Their creation involves vigorous pawing of the ground but no mud-larking is involved. This also applies to the smaller scrapes made by **muntjac** bucks, an activity which may occur at any time of year. In some muntjac areas scrapes are rarely seen but they are more common where the population density is greater and boundary disputes are likely to occur more often.

Gaits

According to *The Guinness Book of Records* the **roe** deer is the fastest British land mammal over a sustained distance, which seems a feasible claim. Unfortunately the text doesn't explain how and where the figures were obtained. A cruising speed of 25-30 m.p.h. with occasional bursts up to 40 m.p.h. also sounds reasonable but monitoring the animal for more than 20 miles is questionable. There are few areas in Britain where a roe is likely to run so far when disturbed.

Radio-tracking studies in Denmark showed that most roe, when startled from cover during hunting, ran between a half and 2 miles, whilst those disturbed by orienteers ran a slightly shorter range of distances; but a red hind ran for nearly 4 miles. Two whole days elapsed before she returned to the area of forest from which she had come. The degree of disturbance and alternative cover available obviously influence the distance the deer run. Greater disturbance would be expected when large orienteering events are held, sometimes with 2,000 runners. Deer are

Roe doe bounding (top), *fallow doe changing from gallop to pronk* (middle) *and red hinds trotting* (below).

designed to cope with escaping from predators but the extra energy expended in fleeing, combined with the loss of time for feeding, could have serious consequences for the deer, especially if the disturbances were frequent or at times of physiological stress, such as when females are lactating or when their fat reserves are at their lowest in late winter.

When a runaway antlered deer, subsequently reported as a red stag, galloped through the streets of Stalybridge in Cheshire in October 1970 the police were ready with their radar trap! He registered 42 m.p.h. Maximum speeds recorded in m.p.h. for other deer are: wapiti 43; reindeer 31; mule deer 34; white-tailed deer 29. Under normal circumstances deer usually walk or trot rather than gallop.

When walking, the left legs perform the same movements as the right legs, but half a stride later. At any one time two, three or, in some deer, four legs may be touching the ground. When trotting, two diagonally opposite legs support the body at a time. If the deer changes to a gallop the right and the left legs are making different movements and at times the body is unsupported, following the push-off by the hind-legs or fore-legs. The gallop may be modified to a bound for which the deer pushes off the ground with both hind-legs and lands on both fore feet. This action is commonly seen in summer when **roe** or **fallow** are moving through tall grass or corn. It is much less frequently used by **muntjac** which, unless frightened, usually potter along at a walking pace.

'Pronking', also known as 'stotting' or 'spronking', is a spectacular gait used quite often by **fallow**. All four feet take off and land together. After take-off the deer rises high in the air, with the legs hanging vertically. Although it is not as fast as the gallop it has some advantages. Change of direction or progress up hill is easily achieved while pronking and the animal is very conspicuous to other fallow, alerting them of the need to

'How does a deer swim without webbed feet?'

flee. Although white-tailed deer don't pronk, their close relation the mule deer do use this style of locomotion. Recent studies on the hybrids of these two species showed that they used a unique escape gait, intermediate between the gallop and the pronk, of the respective parents. Where the natural distributions of the two species overlap, cross-breeding sometimes occurs and it is suspected that the hybrids are less well adapted and less efficient at escaping from predators or other danger.

While the **reindeer** are particularly good swimmers, other species will also swim of necessity or sometimes from choice. When **sika** deer were released on Brownsea Island in 1896 they very soon swam across Poole Harbour to the Dorset coast and there are still movements of sika between the two. **Fallow** have swum between the islets in Loch Lomond; those on Sidney Island in the Strait of Georgia, Canada, swam there from a neighbouring island. Being chased by dogs was sufficient impetus for some fallow to leave Hankø island and head a short distance across Oslo Fjord to the mainland of Norway. **Roe** too can swim well as was seen a few years ago when one was photographed crossing Southampton Water. These are but a few examples, all involving distances up to a few miles.

Where are they?

The maps indicate the approximate distribution of deer in Britain. Sika, roe and muntjac have all extended their distribution considerably in recent years and continue to do so. Escapes from parks or zoos can occur at any time so a species may turn up well outside its usual range. Several years ago while on a road in Deeside, a stronghold for red and roe, I was rather surprised to 'spot one fallow deer in a field with cattle. There was no mistaking it, a white doe. Enquiries revealed that she had been around the area for about twelve years but no one knew from where she had originated. So be prepared for the unexpected.

Some woodlands harbour two or more species of deer. Frequently fallow and muntjac or red and roe occur together and all of these are present in Thetford Forest. One lucky morning I was able to show some visitors all four within ten minutes within one block of the forest. The New Forest is probably the only area to have sika in addition to these four, but the muntjac there are few in number.

Red deer have a predominantly Scottish distribution, mostly in the Highlands in areas known as deer forests of which there are about 160, each of many thousands of acres. The term 'deer forest' is peculiar to Scotland and there may not be a tree in sight! Outside Scotland the herds of red deer are reckoned in dozens or hundreds. Some of the English populations originated from the days of hunting the carted deer which were kept in paddocks or stalls between hunt days when they were

A red deer about to leave the cart at the beginning of a hunt (c. 1912)

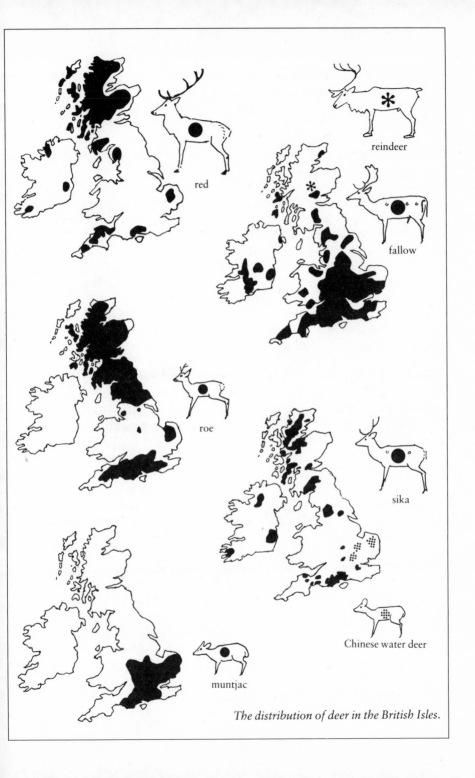

red

reindeer

fallow

roe

sika

Chinese water deer

muntjac

The distribution of deer in the British Isles.

transported in a cart, released and galloped for miles ahead of the horses and hounds. Some were cornered and put back in the cart, others took themselves home and others remained at liberty. The practice mostly had ceased by World War II. Exmoor, the Quantock Hills, New Forest, Thetford Forest and the Lake District all have established populations of red deer and smaller numbers occur in north Essex, Dunwich Forest and elsewhere.

Sika, too, are mainly Scottish in distribution but with other populations in the Ribble Valley of Yorkshire, the Lake District, Hampshire, Dorset, Lundy Island and Ireland. The hurricane of October 1987 gave some park sika the freedom of the Sussex countryside and indeed at that time various species made their exits from enclosures. Most of the stock of sika for Scottish and English parks, from which escapes occurred, came from Co. Wicklow; they were brought to Powerscourt Park about 1860, the first of our Asiatic introductions.

Roe, like red deer, have had a continuous history in Britain since fossil times. By the seventeenth century their numbers had fallen drastically in southern England and they still have a predominantly northern distribution. The present widespread southern populations originate from re-introductions to Dorset, Sussex and the Norfolk/Suffolk border during the 1800s. Their distribution continues to expand and dispersing animals occasionally turn up in urban areas, including Croydon and Bristol.

In contrast, **fallow** are few in Scotland but are established in several areas of the mainland and on Mull, Scarba and Islay. Their wide distribution elsewhere is partly rooted in their presence since Norman times in various English and Irish forests but also reflects their enduring popularity as the favourite park deer. Many of the present-day wild herds originate from park escapes, particularly during the two world wars. Hardly an English county is without feral fallow and they are in six of the eight Welsh counties.

Our two Chinese species owe their origins in England to one estate, Woburn in Bedfordshire. The first records of **muntjac** beyond this area were in the 1920s. Later escapes from Whipsnade and from Hertfordshire boosted the feral populations. Their present distribution reaches to about the northern ends of Lincolnshire and Nottinghamshire with some isolated records from further north. They continue to spread east, west and to the coast of central southern England where any woodland or scrubland offering thick cover and a range of food plants is likely to have a resident population.

Although **water deer** also escaped from Woburn and Whipsnade, their success was far more limited. Some became established in the vicinities but introductions to other counties were of limited success and short duration. They remain our species with the smallest distribution and least numbers. The origin of the present population in the Cambridgeshire fenland is uncertain but those living in the Norfolk Broads are descended from some that came from a private collection in the 1950s. On the day that I write this, a water deer has been killed on a road within Bury St Edmunds, making it the third known record for Suffolk, all of them within three years. The second report was from Minsmere and one presumes the deer had come from the Broads or a captive collection. The most likely origin of the other two was a wildlife park north of Thetford Forest.

The traditional way of bringing shot red deer off the hill in Scotland.

Parks ancient and modern

In Great Britain today there are around 140 deer parks, most of them in England. Forty years ago there were 177, but in 1892 there were 395 in England alone. Even the latter figure was small compared with the number in the hey-day of deer parks in the medieval period. In the early Middle Ages (1086-1485) nearly 2,000 parks for the hunting of deer are known to have existed in England, but not necessarily all at the same time. A map of their distribution looks like England with measles, with Sussex and Essex as the spottiest, both having more than a hundred parks. Over the centuries the purpose of the parks changed and so did the use of the surrounding countryside.

Now some of the large parks such as Richmond, Lyme and Bradgate are close to great conurbations so even town-bound people have the opportunity to become familiar with red and fallow deer. Small paddocks, rather than proper deer parks, also exist in several cities, including London. Sika, muntjac and water deer live in a few parks but roe aren't kept as a park species.

Parks are ideal places for an introduction to the pleasures of deer watching, for the park animals will be more easily seen and more tolerant of voices and movement than their wild cousins. Children should be taught to respect the deer, not to approach too closely, never to run towards them and not to attempt to feed them. It is a great pity that so few parks take the opportunity to inform the public about deer, and other wildlife they contain, by illustrated display boards, guided walks or leaflets.

Many of the long established deer parks have interesting histories which reflect the social and economic changes and customs over the centuries. How many of the thousands of people who daily walk, jog, ride or drive through Richmond Park realize this royal park was created for Charles 1 and that deer hunting with horses and hounds took place there from 1637 until the middle of the following century.

Other royal parks, all with public access, in or near to London still have deer. At Bushy Park and across the road in Home Park, adjacent to Hampton Court, deer graze as they did nearly five centuries ago. Hyde Park, which supplied venison for the monarch's table, ceased to have deer in 1833 when the last remaining deer were transferred to other parks. Their decline in Hyde Park was attributed to dogs, and uncontrolled dogs

• Park Site

The medieval parks of England (from Leonard Cantor).

chasing deer towards cars is a problem now in Richmond Park. Everyone who enters Hyde Park via the Queensgate entrance, near the Royal Albert Hall, sees that the pillars are surmounted by a pair of sculptures of a red hind and her calf. The sculptor, P. Rouillard, must have known deer very well to have captured so accurately and beautifully the postures and attitudes of the animals. The figures were donated anonymously by a French gentleman in 1919. His choice of subject probably had no link with the park's previous use, particularly as it seems only fallow deer had been kept there.

Three parks can be singled out from all the rest. Various chapters in this book make reference to Woburn Park. Until last century it was a typical large 1,000 acre/406 ha. park with red and fallow. Then the Duke of Bedford, and more especially his son, the 11th Duke, became very enthusiastic about introducing exotic animals. From 1895 onwards he imported no less than thirty-seven kinds of deer from around the world. Some were liberated into the park while others needing special care were kept in small enclosures, but even so some, including those from South America, did not thrive. Today Woburn still has a wider range of deer species than any other park. Several hundred Père David deer, about a third of the world's population, share the park (in which they were saved from extinction) with red, sika, fallow, barasingha, muntjac, water deer and a few rusa and axis. The park is also known for the quality of its red and fallow, the males producing good antlers.

Warnham Park in Sussex is not open to the public but its reputation for the finest red deer in Britain is known far and wide. A number of stags have produced over 40 points on their antlers (the record is 47) whereas few Scottish stags attain more than 12 points. Sussex can also claim the

Warnham Park stags under the browse line they created.

most famous park for fallow at Petworth. Here visitors to the National Trust property can see about a thousand of them within the ancient park. This is the largest of our park herds but it is the heavy body weights, coupled with especially broad-palmed antlers, that continues to keep Petworth fallow in demand for stocking other parks and farms.

Deer parks have long been a feature of the landscape, originally as wooded hunting areas and later, in the form we know today, as attractive surroundings for a stately home. The current distribution of fallow is closely associated with the existence of ancient and modern parks. (A list of parks that hold deer is given on p.131).

'Don't go that way if you value your skin.'

Suckers, biters and borers

Deer are host to a number of external parasites, all of which have fascinating life-cycles. Their distribution and prevalence varies a lot in different parts of Britain. Least fussy of all is the tick, which will feed on any deer or indeed almost any of our wild mammals as well as sheep and dogs, even someone handling a deer or walking in areas where they are present. It is as well to recognize this animal, known as the sheep- or deer- or castor-bean-tick, *Ixodes ricinus*. It is the vector for a bacterium which causes Lyme disease in humans, an infection not known until 1975. Possibly a crippling disease of the joints, recorded as 'fillun', which was rife among inhabitants of Jura two hundred years ago, was the same as Lyme disease. The red deer and the ticks are still abundant on this Scottish island.

Not all deer-ticks are carriers and most people who are bitten have no ill effects. The first sign is usually, but not always, a red circular patch of inflammation on the skin around the bite site which increases over several days. Other symptoms are variable and include headache, stiff neck, 'flu-like malaise; subsequently arthritis, meningitis or paralysis may occur and there have even been fatal cases. But don't panic! Early treatment with antibiotics nips Lyme disease in the bud and the important point is for people most at risk to be aware of the potential problem.

The adult female tick feeds on the host's blood. She is mated while feeding, drops off and lays her eggs on the ground. A year later six-legged

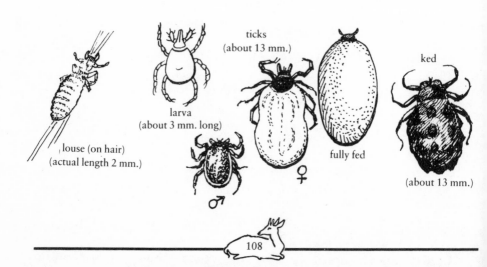

louse (on hair)
(actual length 2 mm.)

larva
(about 3 mm. long)

ticks
(about 13 mm.)

fully fed

♂

♀

ked

(about 13 mm.)

An itchy time for a roe with a high tick burden.

larvae hatch, find a host and have a blood meal. Another year passes before, now as nymphs with the adult's complement of eight legs, they feed on a host for a week. A third year is spent on the ground before moulting into the adult.

The other ectoparasites on deer are all insects. The smallest are the lice, which are wingless. There are two types: biters (of skin debris) and suckers (of blood). Some, like the fallow louse, are very host specific while another is content with red, roe or sika as its restaurant. To spot lice on a deer you usually have to look very carefully, preferably with a hand-lens, in the sparsely haired groins.

Keds are strange-looking flies which appear to have been flattened from top to bottom. Within a day or two of reaching their deer host the wings break off. Then they scuttle about like little crabs among the hairs and feed on blood from the skin.

Far more serious a menace are the warble flies which are active in May and June and make life especially unpleasant for red deer in Scotland. Their eggs are laid on the hairs, the larvae hatch and burrow below the skin on the back, creating bumps through which they will later emerge as adults. The deer warble is a different species from the one that parasitizes cattle and horses. Warbles are absent from New Zealand so the hides from deer there are in very good condition and suitable for manufacture into high quality garments.

Another species of warble parasitizes reindeer (caribou) and in Alaska, Scandinavia and Russia can cause severe debilitation, even leading to death. Between one hundred and two hundred warbles on one reindeer is common but in extreme cases may be ten times as many. Each plump larva is 2.5 mm. (1 in.) long. The discomfort to the reindeer must be intense and there is considerable economic loss in the case of the domesticated herds. Up to thirty per cent reduction in income has been attributed to parasitic insects. In recent years some herds have been treated with a chemical that kills the warble larvae. Often the reindeer respond to the approach of warble or bot-flies by sneezing violently and closing the nostrils repeatedly. Just running away isn't much help — warbles can fly 12-20 miles (20-30 km.)

Equally unpleasant are the nasal bot-flies but, as with all these parasites, one can't but admire their adaptations to their life-styles. The eggs hatch into larvae within the adult female insect. She makes darting flights and rapidly injects the larvae into the deer's nostrils. Here they feed on mucus and blood as they wriggle to their winter quarters, high in the nasal passages. In spring they wriggle back to the nostrils, fall to the ground, pupate and moult to adults. At the very least they cause irritation and at worst they can suffocate the deer by blocking the nasal passages.

By comparison head-flies are relatively harmless but they can be intensely irritating as they swarm round the face and velvet antlers. They feed on sweat and secretions from the eyes and mouth; only the females will drink blood. Seeking windier spots, mud wallows and rubbing posts gives the deer a little relief.

A fallow doe having a good scratch.

Natural mortality

In Britain natural death of deer is mostly the result of starvation, severe weather, parasites, disease or old age. The first two are common among the Highland red deer and relatively rare for other species down south. Many of the red deer are living on the edge of their range, in a bleak environment where winter shortage of food is common because there are more deer than the vegetation can support and access to sheltered areas is in some places barred by forest fences. If March and April bring heavy rain and chilling winds the already weakened deer succumb and spring mortalities can reach unacceptable figures. The first few weeks of life are also a very vulnerable period. On Rhum a fifth of the calves born in June had died by the end of September, the majority within a week of birth.

Fighting between males can result in one piercing the other with the point of an antler, or slashing him with a tusk in the case of muntjac or water deer. Infection may enter or the wound may become fly-blown. During a fight occasionally the two males get their antlers so interlocked that neither can free himself, so both starve to death, locked in mortal combat. Such cases have been reported in roe, fallow, sika, the hog deer of Indonesia, white tails, mule deer and no doubt some others too. A skilful Danish deer-keeper at the large deer park close to Copenhagen was once able to save two fallow bucks from this horrid fate by shooting a piece off one antler, sufficient for the bucks to disengage and live to fight another day.

In some localities the burden of internal parasites may cause deaths whereas the same parasite may be absent in another population of deer of the same species. For instance, roe deer in Dorset and Hampshire often have very heavy burdens of lungworms but roe in the Breckland rarely have any. These parasites look like short pieces of white cotton. When large numbers are present they can block the airways to the extent of causing suffocation. More often they cause damage to the lung tissue which becomes susceptible to invasion by pathogens from which the deer may die.

Of all our deer, the roe is also the most susceptible to liverfluke and some natural deaths can be attributed to this parasite, which also affects sheep and cattle. Argyllshire is one region where heavy infestation has been found in roe. The complex life history of the fluke involves one stage in a particular species of snail, so if the environment is not right for the

Double danger.

snail there won't be a liverfluke problem in that locality.

Intestinal worms are rarely a problem in deer: the number they have is generally much lower than in cattle and sheep. The larval stage of a tapeworm may be found in a deer carcase, usually attached to the gut or wall of the abdominal cavity. They look like a soft, milky-white marble or may be the size of a ping-pong ball. They can occur in any species of deer although I have yet to find one in a muntjac. During a survey of the incidence of this bladderworm cyst, as the larva is called, 12 per cent of over 300 fallow in southern England had one to three cysts, but in such small numbers the cysts will not harm the deer. Before the life-cycle can progress to the adult stage, a tapeworm, the cyst must be eaten by a carnivore, usually a fox or a dog. So a stalker should be wary of discarding entrails where his dog may consume them.

There are a number of bacterial and viral diseases that can affect deer but the incidence seems to be low. As far as we know at present they seldom constitute an important cause of mortality in wild populations. The growth of deer farming has encouraged studies on deer diseases, for any such problems are usually intensified under captive conditions.

Predators

In Britain the only wild mammals to prey on deer are foxes. Some of the remains found at their earths will be of still-births or aborted foetuses, but they can take live deer. The extent of this predation is not known but a study in Sweden estimated that five to ten kids and one adult roe were taken by foxes within about 2,500 acres (1,000 ha.) during May-August, but no distinction could be made between those taken alive and those taken as carrion.

A female deer with young can be a formidable opponent to anyone or any carnivore attempting to take her youngster. She will flail her sharp front hooves at the intruder or give chase if she is not within striking distance. I've known someone intervene to retrieve a roe kid carried off by a fox. The kid had tooth-puncture wounds and died despite receiving veterinary attention. Had it survived, what would the rescuer have done with a hand-tame roe buck? Much better to have let nature take its course. In Sweden, in severe winters when deep snow made voles inaccessible, foxes ate more roe, but the proportion of those that had starved to death and those caught while in a weakened condition could not be determined.

Unfortunately dogs account for a number of deaths of deer. The temptation to chase and strike an animal running across a park or through a wood is too great for most dogs, hence the bye-law in many state forests

A roe doe in defence of her kid.

Don't let dogs chase deer.

to keep dogs under control. While muntjac are particularly vulnerable to these attacks, because of their small size, red and fallow in public parks may be harassed many times in a single day.

In Scotland some roe kids and red calves are taken by golden eagles. In former times wolves were the major predator of deer in many countries including Britain. Studies in North America have shown how efficient wolves are at selecting weak, injured or old caribou from the herd. Unfortunately there are very few places in Europe, but the Carpathian Mountains in eastern Europe is one, where the wolf remains a significant predator on roe and red deer. In Scandinavia wolverines, lynx, bears and eagles prey on reindeer. Axis deer is a relatively easy prey for tigers in India but they will also take barasingha and sambar.

Hunters were so concerned at the risk of competition between themselves and pumas for the black-tailed deer in Washington State that between 1905 and 1961 a bounty scheme was in operation. It was estimated that one puma would kill 20 deer a year. Since puma control stopped the number of deer shot has decreased by 14 per cent, but many factors could be involved. Even if a rise in puma numbers was the main reason, with an annual harvest of over 60,000 black-tails one would expect the hunters to be content. In Montana a survey of 87 carcases of white-tails and mule deer showed that coyotes and pumas had accounted for 15 and 18 per cent respectively, but 67 per cent were road kills.

Most European countries and American States compile figures for road traffic accidents involving deer. Sweden, for example, has recorded 10,000 moose, red and roe killed on the roads in one year. There are no figures available for Britain as a whole but in the New Forest alone about 80, and in Cannock Chase over 50, are known to be killed in a year, and they are just two of our 'good' deer areas.

Such accidents are no replacement for natural control by predators. They are unselective and many of the deer are not killed outright but receive injuries which may cause prolonged suffering before death. Some survive despite major damage: three-legged fallow does have been found to be pregnant when killed in later accidents. Of 111 fallow road casualties in Essex the number of males and females was virtually equal but in the rutting season (October-November) the number of bucks killed was significantly higher than at any other time. In a sample of over 60 muntjac road kills from one area of Suffolk their ages ranged from four months to over ten years, but there were twice as many males as females.

Roe and fallow born in grass fields are at considerable risk from mowing machines and their natural 'sitting tight' strategy is no protection from this 'predator'. For such accidents in this country no figures are available (as I seem to say so often) but a study in an intensively cultivated area of west Poland calculated that twenty-six per cent of the roe kids born were lost to agricultural machinery. Of greater concern than the outright deaths are the animals maimed by farm machinery. All too often a limb is severed. Euthanasia is usually the kindest course of action.

Another risk to roe that feed in cultivated fields has a less direct link with man's activities. In Germany, Austria and the east of Scotland there

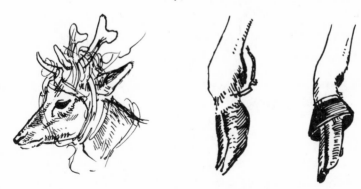

Hazards for fallow and other deer include plastic baler twine, fox snares and lost lens hoods.

have been deaths of roe that had eaten a particular variety of oil-seed rape called 00 (Double Zero).

Trains claim a few lives as deer cross railway lines, and some deer, mostly roe, endure a lingering death when their legs become caught by the strands of barbed-wire fence. Another man-made hazard for some Scottish red deer that feed on seaweed are the fishing nets that are washed ashore. Their feet and antlers can become entangled. A similar result can occur when plastic baler twine is discarded on farmland where inquisitive antlered deer can become festooned with it.

Longevity

Ancient beliefs in the longevity of deer were widespread and symbolic statues of sika deer, representing health and long life, can be seen in many towns in China today, as well as at the Imperial Palace in Beijing. According to one version of a classical legend, a crow lived three times the life of a man and a stag three lives of a crow. These are gross exaggerations, but if a deer survives its early, most vulnerable period of life it has the potential to live a good many years. Its chances of making old bones will vary with its locality, some habitats being more hazardous than others.

Twenty years is on record for the life-span of a captive **fallow** and this was the age of a white-lipped stag living in Shanghai Zoo in 1988. Some **red** deer on Rhum attain this age although only a few hinds calve after 13 years. In Richmond Park a red hind was still breeding when 18 years old; her exact age was known because, like the Rhum deer, she had been ear-tagged as a calf. For the majority of Scottish red deer life is much shorter. Estimates indicate that 50 per cent survive until their fourth year and only 25 per cent reach their eighth year. Possibly the world record for a red deer goes to a hand-reared Scottish hind still alive after 27 years.

A long-term study of **roe** deer in Dorset showed that a few reached 12 years but 95 per cent of the population died by their eighth year. Longevity records for captive **muntjac** are 19 years for a doe and over 16 years for a buck. Wild muntjac, tagged when of adult size but unknown age, have been found about 10 years later when hit by a vehicle.

Why control?

Seeing deer in our parks or countryside gives a lot of pleasure to many people. Some of them become upset when a number of deer are shot just because there are too many deer, not because they are injured or aged, although these categories should be the first to be culled. In the absence of natural predators man must intervene and manage the deer, limiting their number to that which the land can support adequately or to a level at which the damage inflicted upon crops (which include timber) is tolerable. The actual number will vary enormously according to the vegetation (which in turn depends upon soil, climate, topography and any management regimes), the presence or absence of other large herbivores (cattle, sheep, other deer), any crops being grown and the species of deer under consideration.

The purpose for which the deer are maintained may be purely aesthetic — they look pretty in a park — so the ratio of the sexes is not very important; but if they are kept primarily for venison production a preponderance of females is required. If stalking for trophy heads is the main desire then a good supply of males of the older ages will be needed.

Even allowing for some natural mortality and accidental deaths, numbers of deer can build up very significantly in a few years. The carrying capacity of the land may increase temporarily in some circumstances, as in certain stages of the growth of a coniferous forest, but usually it is limited. If the vegetation becomes over-grazed it will be less productive and not have a chance to recover in the continued presence of deer. More deer trying to live off less vegetation leads to poor body condition, lower weights and increased parasite burdens. For the welfare of the deer (as well as commercial reasons) it is far better to manage the deer so there is plenty of food for a smaller number of strong animals.

In most parks counting deer is relatively easy, especially if supplementary feed is provided in winter and the deer assemble at a few spots where hay, roots or cereals are distributed. In the wild, red, fallow and sika often move over land owned by several people. Owner A may see a herd of forty deer on his fields one week and decide to cull ten as soon as the open shooting season begins. Owners B, C and D may see the same herd on their lands and come to the same decision. If they all acted independently the whole population could be shot, which was not what any of them intended. In practice it is unlikely to work out like that but this example shows the need for landowners to co-operate and co-ordinate, to census the deer population common to their various properties, which means knowing their movements. Management groups are set up for these purposes, and some estates appoint a deer manager or consultant to draw up a cull plan, taking into account the various age categories of each sex within the total population. There is much more to proper deer management than pulling a trigger.

In Britain landowners can decide how many deer they, or stalkers appointed by them, are to shoot on their own land. There is no licence from any department or organization stipulating how many deer they are permitted to take, but the law does regulate close seasons and permitted weapons. Many countries and states do have such a regulation and details of animals shot have to be submitted to a game or wildlife department, sometimes with a jaw (for estimation of the age of the deer); in other places the antlers have to be exhibited. The data received by such departments are used to assess trends in body weights, antler sizes, reproductive rate, age structure and the total population.

When a report was compiled a few years ago for the United Nations Environment Programme on the status of European and North American deer, Great Britain was one of the countries with the least data available. No estimates existed for our total populations of roe, fallow and sika. Within state forests around 12,000 roe are shot annually but roe occur in many areas not under the control of the Forestry Commission and a recent estimate suggested a total of 200,000. The red deer in Scotland are the only populations for which annual estimates are available.

The Red Deer Commission (RDC), set up in 1959 with responsibility for the conservation and control of red deer in Scotland, sends a census team of eight or ten men to each of forty-five blocks which together cover most of the open deer country in Scotland. Deer within fenced forests are not included but details of those shot are submitted to the RDC. Each of the blocks is sub-divided into areas which are surveyed on successive days. On a favourable day, which usually means the weather is harsh enough to have brought the deer down to the lower ground and they stand out well against the snow, the team may survey 50,000 acres (20,250 ha.). From the census figure the RDC advises the landowner of the recommended cull for stags, hinds and calves. For some years now many estates have failed to achieve the cull figure advised for hinds. There is more attraction in shooting stags and guest stalkers will pay for the privilege. Other factors come into the story too, one being the short duration of the open season for hinds — about a hundred working days in the months with least day-

Breaching the forest fence.

length and often poor visibility. Whatever the reasons, the red deer population has escalated to over 300,000.

England now has large stocks of deer of several species, but no one has estimates of how many. They impinge upon many interests and activities such as farming, forestry, road construction and nature conservation. Government departments or their agencies involved with agriculture, forestry, road and airport safety, environmental matters and firearms all become involved with a diverse range of problems associated with deer. Perhaps the time will come when England has an organization whose role would be to gather and collate relevant data about its deer populations.

Deterrents

Some gardeners are prepared to swap roses for roe, but others do not want their treasured plants or new trees to be eaten; various barriers or deterrents have been used. Mesh fencing is only economically justifiable for large-scale afforestation. Very precise specifications must be given for its erection because deer are skilled fence-breakers as well as jumpers. It has been said that a red hind, the largest of our female deer, can push through a hole 20 cm. (8 in.) wide.

Electric fencing is appropriate in some situations but it must be made very visible to the deer to avoid the risk of entanglement. Muntjac have been known to get caught in the modern mesh electric fencing, erected to contain sheep. In deer parks wooden or wood and metal tree cradles have been used very satisfactorily to protect newly planted trees. The modern plastic tree guards are in effect a lighter-weight, shorter-term version of these cradles.

Apart from these physical barriers, searches have been made for chemicals that will, by their smell or taste, deter deer from browsing the trees on which the substances have been sprayed, painted or smeared. Several brands of chemicals are available. Most are used in winter, before the most vulnerable season. Applications on a large scale are labour intensive, especially as they need to be repeated.

The smell of creosote is a temporary deterrent and similar claims have been made for human hair! The long-standing joke that lion dung could be an effective deterrent has progressed to a reality. Although nowadays normally no deer would ever meet a lion it seems that no other carnivore's excrement will do, except in North America where puma dung deters white-tailed deer. The active ingredient of lion dung has been isolated and synthesized in sufficient quantities for extensive field trials of a spray containing synthetic essence of lion dung. The final product is eagerly awaited by foresters, farmers and gardeners.

Deer farming

Venison has long been prized as a fine meat worthy of the nobility. Richmond Park still annually supplies haunches to the holders of certain high offices of state, a remnant of the centuries old custom of the Royal Venison Warrants.

Deer farming began in Britain in 1970 and now pre-packed venison is available in many supermarkets. Of the several hundred farms, most are stocked with red deer, some with fallow. Many of the Scottish farms sell weaned calves in the autumn, when they weigh about 30 kg. (66 lb.), to farmers further south where the pastures are better. The males are kept until the following summer or autumn, being slaughtered at about 100 kg. (220 lb.). Females are kept for breeding. There is an export market to eastern Asia for by-products such as testes, penises, sinews and tails.

The rise of deer farming has coincided with a greater awareness of what we eat and concern over husbandry methods used for some of the more traditional food animals. Deer farmers point out that their venison, which is always tender because the animals are slaughtered when young, is a lean meat, low in cholesterol and free of additives.

The Chinese medicine chest

The farming of deer for a different purpose has a much longer history in the East, perhaps having begun over 2,000 years ago in China. Today that country and Russia farm vast numbers of deer, mostly sika, because deer are the most used of all animals in Chinese traditional medicine.

Nearly thirty different parts of the body or their products are used to treat or prevent numerous conditions, especially those associated with fertility and senescence. The venison is usually dried and used to make a wine, then re-dried and ground to a powder to make tonic pills, but the greatest demand is for thin slices of velvet-covered growing antlers. The antlers are sawn off, a practice prohibited in Britain. In New Zealand where deer farms export large quantities of velvet antlers to the eastern markets, the law requires that an anaesthetic be administered to the stags before their antlers are removed. Cutting off hard antlers, which are then dead bone and therefore incapable of feeling pain, is a completely different matter and is normal procedure in Britain if mature males have to be transported.

Lore unto themselves

From the earliest of times man has incorporated deer into art, religion, superstition, myth and legend. Red and reindeer were shown on Stone Age cave paintings in southern Europe, reindeer and moose appear on Scandinavian rock carvings, fallow feature on the oldest known inscribed coin and Persian fallow are woven on the oldest known carpet, to give but a few examples.

All manner of craftsmen over the millennia have used deer in their creations. Some representations are stylized, like the stag on King Redwald's sceptre found in the Sutton Hoo ship burial, the richest Anglo-Saxon burial ever found. Other portrayals are more detailed, like the fallow buck's head which forms an exquisite, gold wine-drinking vessel which had been buried in central Bulgaria since the third century BC, but had probably been made hundreds of years earlier. The details of the

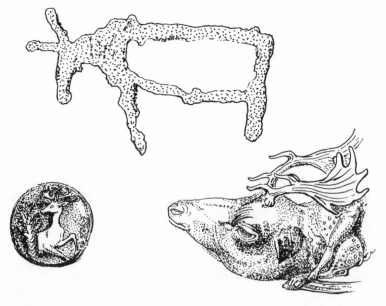

(Above) *Ancient rock carving of a moose in the vicinity of a series of pit-fall traps in Norway.* (Below left) *fallow buck on a Greek coin from Ephesus, 4th century BC;* (below right) *Detail from a 3rd century BC gold vessel from Thrace.*

palms even depict the pattern of grooves left on the surface of an antler by the blood vessels which are present during its growth.

Many animal legends of the classical world were recorded by Aristotle (384-322 BC) and Pliny the Elder (AD 23-79), and later generations perpetuated the stories. Even in Elizabethan England it was written that a stag wounded by an arrow would seek a particular plant, dittany, and be healed.

Pliny referred to swine and stags eating crabs when feeling ill. Pigs are omnivores so crustacea would not be inappropriate in their diet and there could be a grain of truth in deer eating crabs. Scottish red deer with access to seaweed eat it and no doubt there are some dead shore crabs amongst the fronds. The shells of these crustacea are rich in calcium and could be an appropriate dietary supplement.

We should not forget that much of what Aristotle wrote had a correct biological basis. For instance, he knew that deer were among the few mammals to lack a gall bladder. He also recorded the fact that stags castrated while they were young did not grow antlers and that castration after antler development prevented the normal antler cycle.

The ancient belief that deer would fight with and eat snakes was very widely held. The deer were said to put their nostrils to the holes in which snakes hid and draw them out with their breath. One of the platters of the Mildenhall Treasure, the finest hoard of Roman silver tableware ever discovered, shows just such a scene with a red hind close to a snake which is emerging from a pile of rocks. A wood carving in Ely cathedral illustrates the snake-eating habit, which was supposed to enable the deer to gain a new lease of life: another thread in the longevity legend.

A red hind drawing out a snake from its hiding place (4th century AD Roman platter, Mildenhall Treasure).

Having had its reptilian repast the deer quickly had to drink, else it was doomed. This association of ideas was taken up in some of the bestiaries, those early natural history books, often lavishly illustrated, in which characteristics attributed to real or fabulous animals were used to teach morals and Christian doctrine. Thus the stag represented the Christian who fights sin (the serpent) and rushes to the water for baptism.

The snake story was still sufficiently in vogue in the fourteenth century for the Knights of the Order of St John of Jerusalem to introduce fallow deer to Rhodes to stamp out snakes. Maybe that was just a pretext, for they also established a deer forest for their own sport. Wild and captive fallow still live on the island for which the deer became the symbol, hence the bronze statues of a buck and doe which stand on columns either side of the Mandraki Harbour, which in ancient times was straddled by the Colossus. But in other places it is the snakes that attack the deer. In India rat snakes are known to take muntjac fawns; in North America prairie rattle-snakes have bitten captive Rocky Mountain wapiti and no doubt young brockets are welcome fare for anacondas.

Medieval art and literature make references to weeping deer, probably because the secretion from the sub-orbital glands have been mistaken for tears. Usually these secretions are thick and, certainly in fallow and red deer, can become quite firm, brown pellets. In some instances they may have been mistaken for bezoar stones. The latter are stony concretions which sometimes form in the stomach of ruminants and were widely believed to be an antidote to any poison. The pampas deer was especially associated with these stones, to the extent of being named after them, *Ozotoceros bezoarticus*. Within the last hundred years some pampas deer were killed for these stones, prized for medicinal and superstitious reasons. The extensive use of many parts of deer in eastern medicine is mentioned on page 121.

Another superstition caused the unfortunate infants of the Eskimo people of St Lawrence Island, south of the Bering Strait, to be subjected to an itchy experience. For the first two years of life the child had to wear a tight-fitting hood made of deerskin, to prevent its head growing too big! This custom was still being observed at the end of the last century.

A cervine version of the Pied Piper story was related in the seventeenth century. A score of fallow bucks were said to have been led by a bag-piper some two hundred miles from Yorkshire to Hampton Court. When the music stopped, so did the deer, but they walked on as soon as the piper resumed playing. At that time and until much later it was normal practice to lead cattle, sheep and geese long distances by road, but without musical accompaniment.

Transports of delight

Reindeer are the only deer to be used regularly as draught animals. In many of the northern latitudes where they pull sledges no other animal could perform the task. The association between Santa Claus and reindeer apparently began in a poem, 'A visit from St Nicholas', written in 1823. The poet, the Rev. Clement More, conceived the idea of Santa's sleigh being drawn by reindeer and this was first illustrated by Thomas Nast.

In the eighteenth century, when horse-drawn carriages were the normal mode of transport for the gentry, the Earl of Orford's phaeton must have caused a stir as it rumbled past. Instead of sturdy steeds he had four stags. Apparently all went well until, while driving through Newmarket, he met a pack of hounds. The stags took fright but fortunately the Earl was able to drive into the yard of a pub which then was called the Ram but is now the Rutland Arms. Someone closed the gates before the hounds could enter. Ludwig VIII rumbled around Baden in a carriage drawn by six stags. A more modest mode of transport, a buggy pulled by one stag, greeted visitors to Linton, Victoria, soon after deer had been introduced to that part of Australia early this century.

An even stranger spectacle was witnessed in France in 1817 when Margat, evidently an eccentric and flamboyant character, decided to out-do another balloonist who, some years earlier, had ascended while on horse-back. Margat, clad in his full dragoon's uniform, sat on his pet stag, named Coco, and was hoisted up by balloon. One hopes the antler tips didn't puncture the balloon.

The Earl of Orford's team.

We're only here for the deer

Nearly every English town seems to have its White Hart, one of the commonest of all pub names. Hart is an almost obsolete word now among the deer-stalking fraternity but meant a red stag of six or more years old. A few hostelries, as in Newmarket, have a stone figure of a stag surmounted by genuine antlers. Some inns show a fallow deer. A particularly fine figure of a buck stands on the portico of a hotel in Salisbury but he cast one antler out of the normal season, during strong February winds!

The White Hart, Salisbury, before he cast an antler.

The name originated in the fourteenth century when Richard II, a popular king, chose a white hart as his badge. About the same time his future father-in-law, Charles VI of France, adopted a white hart as his symbol, but this one had wings. Legend tells that Charles had encountered a white stag wearing a collar which bore an inscription saying that Caesar had collared him. There are also Greek tales as far back as the third century BC which mention deer with collars, so perhaps twentieth century biologists were not the first to mark red deer in this way! Many of the pub signs show the animal wearing a collar, often in the form of a coronet.

To the White Hart in Scole, Norfolk, goes the distinction of having had erected, in the seventeenth century, the largest, most elaborate and expensive inn sign ever created. Two dozen scenes were carved on the beams that spanned the road for 140 years. Today a more modest wrought-iron sign hangs from the wall of what is now called the Scole Inn.

Other deer enticing people to quench their thirst include the Red Hart, Golden Hart, Roebuck, Reindeer, Deer's Leap, White Stag, Bald-faced Stag (which has a white blaze on the head), Bald Hind, Hind's Head, Red Deer, Buck, Running Buck and several other Bucks in company with other animals or a tree, and Buck in the Park.

Saintly stags

When Hubert, the eldest son of the Duke of Aquitaine, went hunting in the Ardennes Forest one Good Friday he was confronted by a magnificent stag. Between its antlers was a radiant crucifix. Hubert was so overcome by its warning of damnation that he renounced his inheritance, but not his love of hunting, took Holy Orders and later, in 727 AD, became Bishop of Liège. Hunters adopted him as their patron saint and an internationally recognized club for stalkers bears his name.

An art gallery isn't a usual place to find a relic of a saint but a hunting horn attributed to St Hubert is in the Wallace Collection in London. Its history has been traced from 1468, when it left Liège, until 1879 when Sir Richard Wallace purchased it. Much of the original seventh-century ox-horn has been covered by fifteenth-century ornamentation, added at a time when pilgrims associated the horn with a cure for rabies. In Idsworth, Hampshire, there is a chapel dedicated to St Hubert. Here a mural, dating from c.1300, shows him curing a man who believed he was a wolf; his encounter with the stag is shown in stained glass, as it is in Herringswell, Suffolk, and elsewhere.

A very similar version is attributed to St Eustace who is said to have been a Roman general, although his existence at all is in some doubt. Although the St Hubert version is now much better known, it is believed that Eustace's legend was incorporated into Hubert's story, but not until the fourteenth century. Such borrowing of tales was not uncommon amongst medieval biographers of saints! The name of the small Norfolk town of East Dereham is derived

St Hubert's horn.

from 'deor', meaning a deer or wild animal. The town's further association with deer is depicted on the carving which spans the main street. Witheburga, eldest daughter of King Anna of the East Angles, became a nun after her father's death in 654 AD. She commanded the building of a church at Dereham but was worried because she had insufficient food for her workmen. In a dream she was told that two does in milk would meet her maids by the river and 'so give comfort to your band'. When a steward of a local manor tried to capture the deer he was thrown from his horse and broke his neck. A document dating from about 1169, some 400 years after the supposed event, is the first known written account. If the translation to 'does' is correct, then the deer at St. Witheburga's time would have been roe, fallow not yet having been reintroduced. The deer on the sign, which was erected in 1954, most closely resemble red deer hinds.

The best known tale associated with St Kentigern (alias Mungo) concerns a lost ring, later recovered in a fish and featured on the arms of the City of Glasgow, but another story claims that he harnessed a stag to a plough. Other saints sometimes depicted with a stag are St Julian Hospitaller, St Felix of Valois, St Aidan, St Godric, St Cairan and St Cainnic.

Deer in the dictionary

Quite a few words and phrases involving deer have crept into our language. In the Oxford English Dictionary almost five columns of text are listed under 'stag', and 'buck' has well over six columns of meanings, examples and explanations.

The word 'buck' used to describe a dashing, dandy fellow with a spirit of gaiety who could well be likened to a fallow buck flaunting himself in the rut. 'To pass the buck' is a frequently used phrase on both sides of the Atlantic which seems to have evolved from a remark by President Truman, '. . . the buck stops here'. 'A buck' as slang for a dollar has a direct connection with deer, dating back to the early days of trading between American Indians and the immigrant settlers. The trade in buck skins, from white-tailed deer, was of major importance and their price remained sufficiently stable to provide a consistent unit of exchange which the merchants called a buck.

'Stag' also once had a monetary

A dashing, dandy buck.

meaning in Britain, but one that is lost and gone forever. A century ago twenty stag meant a shilling. Any connection with deer seems doubtful but stag was also the name for males of various poultry kept for breeding, including cockerels and turkeys. Perhaps the 'twenty stag' was associated with bets on cock-fights which were also called stag-fights.

Around two hundred years ago the term 'stag' was applied to any animal castrated after maturity, a meaning in complete contrast to that given above for poultry! Nor does it link up with the idea of a virile, rutting stag. The word was also applied to a woman of a bold or romping type.

In the USA 'stag' was the name given to a man who attended a social function without a female partner. From this arose 'stag parties', intended for men only. Not until later did stag nights become especially associated with a bridegroom's pre-wedding celebration. Perhaps the name derived from the fact that stags of the red deer and their bigger American cousins, the wapiti, live separately from the females outside the rutting season.

The jargon of the Stock Exchange includes a trio of beasts

Stag party.

of which the Bull and the Bear come from proverbs or a fable. The Stag (one who applies for new stock or shares with the plan of selling at a profit straight away upon receipt, without holding for investment) has a completely different origin. Stag Alley in London was where new issues were announced. But why was the alley so called? Did cock-fights take place there? The verb 'to stag' seems to have been used in this context, meaning to find, follow, observe, discover, shadow or act as a stag on the Stock Exchange.

Today anyone who is humiliated has to eat only a metaphorical portion of humble pie. In medieval times this was a real pie made from the entrails, kidneys, heart and liver of a deer, which collectively were known as 'umbles' or 'humbles'. The dish was served to the hunt servants after a day's sport, while the nobility dined on venison.

Useful information

PARKS AND ENCLOSURES WITH DEER

Parks that are never open to the public have been omitted. Of those listed some are open daily, some only for the summer season and others only occasionally, and arrangements may be liable to alteration, so you are advised to check before a visit. Zoos and wildlife parks have been excluded although many include deer among the species exhibited. At some deer farms there are viewing facilities.

Avon
Ashton Court, Bristol

Bedfordshire
Woburn, Leighton Buzzard

Berkshire
Englefield House, Theale
Great Park, Windsor

Buckinghamshire
Fawley Hill, Henley-on-Thames
Waddesdon Manor, Aylesbury

Cheshire
Lyme, Disley
Tatton, Knutsford

Cornwall
Boconnoc, Lostwithiel

Cumbria
Dalemain, Penrith
Holker Hall, Cark-in-Cartmel
Levens Hall, Kendal

Derbyshire
Chatsworth, Bakewell

Devonshire
Powderham, Exeter

Durham
Raby Castle, Staindrop

Essex
Bedford's, Havering-atte-Bower
St Osyth Priory, Clacton

Gloucestershire
Whitcliff, Berkeley
Lydney, Chepstow

Greater London
Bushy, Teddington
Home Park, Hampton Court
Richmond
Battersea, SW8 ⎫
Clissold, N16 ⎪
Golders Hill, NW3 ⎬ small enclosures
Greenwich, SE10 ⎪
Maryon, SE7 ⎪
Victoria, E9 ⎭

131

Greater Manchester
Dunham Massey, Altrincham

Hampshire
Stratfield Saye Country Park

Hereford and Worcester
Eastnor Castle, Ledbury
Spetchley, Worcester

Hertfordshire
Knebworth, Stevenage

Humberside
Normanby, Scunthorpe
Sewerby, Bridlington

Kent
Boughton Monchelsea, Maidstone
Knole, Sevenoaks
Mersham Hatch, Ashford

Leicestershire
Bradgate, Newtown Linford
Donington, Castle Donington

Lincolnshire
Belton, Grantham

Norfolk
Holkham, Wells-next-the-Sea
Houghton, King's Lynn

North Yorkshire
Studley Royal, Ripon

Nottinghamshire
Thoresby, Ollerton
Wollaton, Nottingham

Oxfordshire
Magdalen College, Oxford
Stonor, Henley-on-Thames

Shropshire
Attingham, Shrewsbury
Weston, Shifnal, Wolverhampton

Somerset
Hatch Court, Taunton
Combe Sydenham, Watchet

Suffolk
Helmingham, Stowmarket
Ickworth, Bury St Edmunds

Warwickshire
Charlecote, Warwick

West Midlands
Birmingham Nature Centre

West Sussex
Leonardslee, near Horsham
Petworth

West Yorkshire
Lotherton Hall, Aberford
Temple Newsom, Leeds

Wiltshire
Dyrham, Chippenham

WALES
W. Glamorgan
Margam Country Park, Port Talbot

SCOTLAND
Angus
Kinnaird Castle, Brechin

Ayrshire
Culzean Country Park, Maybole

Dumfries
Millgreen, Dumfries

Inverness-shire
Reindeer Reserve, Aviemore

Kirkcudbrightshire
Clatteringshaws, Broloch Hill

Strathclyde
Placerigg Country Park, Cumbernauld

West Lothian
Hopetoun House, South Queensferry

IRELAND
Co. Antrim
Randalstown Forest Deer Park
Shane's Castle, Antrim

Co. Dublin
Phoenix Park, Dublin

Co.Monaghan
Lough Fea, Carrickmacross

Co. Roscommon
Lough Key Forest Park, Boyle

Co.Tyrone
Gortin Glen Forest Park, Omagh
Parkanaur Forest, Castlecaulfield

ORGANIZATIONS

The British Deer Society
Beale Centre
Lower Basildon
Reading
Berkshire RG8 9NH

The Mammal Society
Dept. of Zoology
University of Bristol
Bristol BS8 1UG

The British Deer Farmers Association
Holly Lodge
Spencers Lane
Berkswell
Coventry
CV7 7BZ

Red Deer Commission
Inverness
Scotland

Reindeer Council of the U.K.
(including Adopt-a-Reindeer Scheme)
Reindeer House
Aviemore
Inverness-shire
Scotland

Further reading

Bang, P., and P. Dahlstrom, *Collins Guide to Animal Tracks and Signs* (Collins, London, 1990)

British Deer Society: booklets on each of the species in Britain, except reindeer (1980s)

Brown, Michael Baxter, *Richmond Park: the History of a Royal Deer Park* (Robert Hale, London, 1974)

Cantor, L., *The Medieval Parks of England: A Gazetteer* (Loughborough University, Loughborough, 1983)

Caughley, G., *The Deer Wars: The Story of Deer in New Zealand* (Heinemann, London, 1983)

Chapman, Donald & Norma, *Fallow Deer: Their history, distribution and biology* (Terence Dalton, Lavenham, 1975)

Chapman, Norma, *Fallow Deer* (available from Mammal Society, 1984)

Clutton-Brock, J., *Excavations at Grimes Graves, Norfolk, 1972-6* (British Museum Publications, London, 1984)

Clutton-Brock, T.H., F. Guinness and S.D. Albon, *Red Deer: Behavior and Ecology of Two Sexes* (Edinburgh University Press, Edinburgh, 1982)

Corbet, G., and S. Harris (eds), *Handbook of British Mammals* (Blackwells Scientific Publications, Oxford, 1991)

Fletcher, Nichola, *Venison: Monarch of the Table* (1983)

HMSO: booklets by the Forestry Commission on *Fallow Deer, High Seats, Deer Repellents* and *The Management of Red Deer in Upland Forests*

Holmes, Frank, *Following the Roe. A Natural History of the roe deer* (Bartholomew, Edinburgh, 1974)

Leader-Williams, N., *Reindeer on South Georgia: The ecology of an introduced population* (Cambridge University Press, Cambridge, 1988)

Prior, R., *The Roe Deer of Cranborne Chase* (O.U.P., London, 1968)

Putman, Rory, *The Natural History of Deer* (Christopher Helm, Bromley, 1988)

Whitehead, G.K., *The Deer of Great Britain and Ireland. An account of their history, status and distribution* (Routledge & Kegan Paul, London, 1964). Status and distribution have changed but this remains the most comprehensive account of the history of deer in each county.

Whitehead, G.K., *Deer of the World* (Constable, London, 1972)

Index